WEST PC

THE MAKING OF LEADERS

AN HISTORICAL SKETCHBOOK

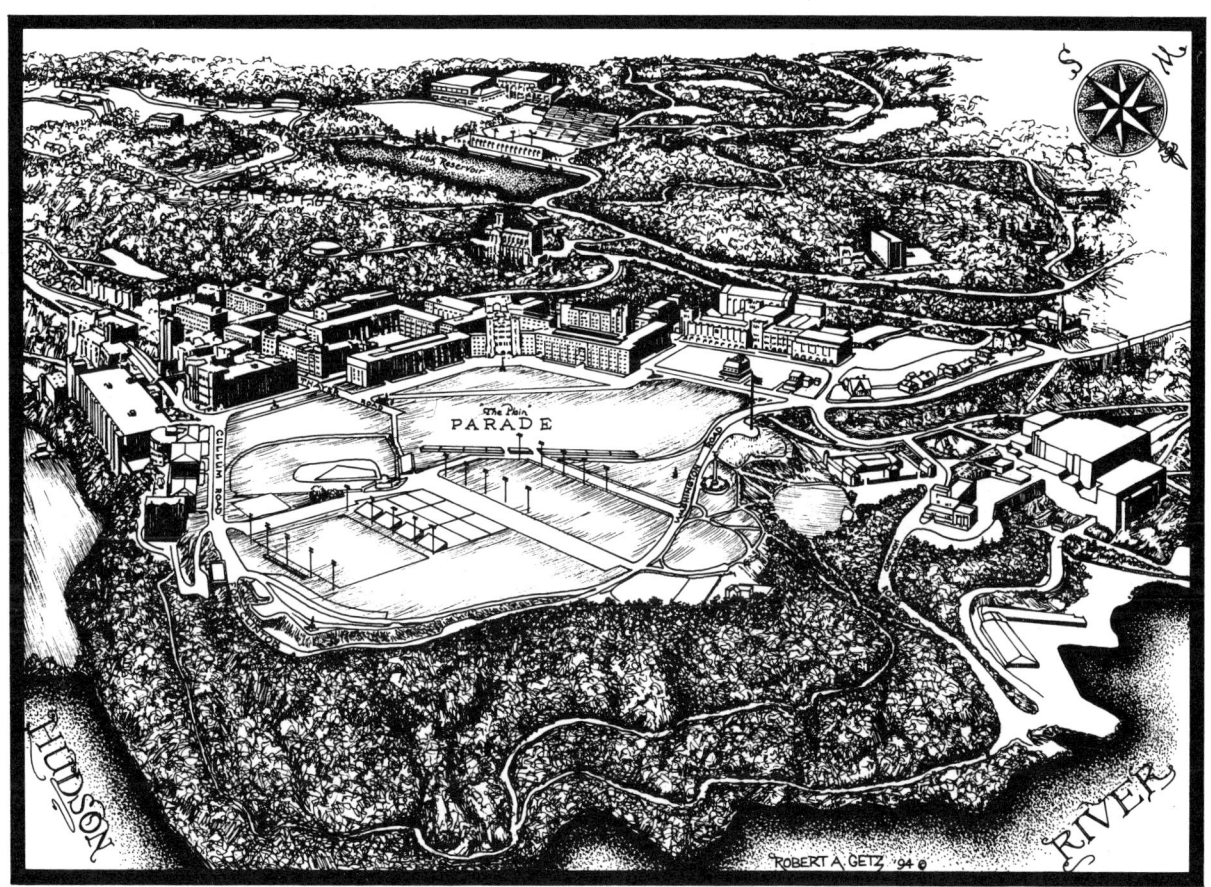

Original pen and ink drawings by   *Robert A. Getz*

Historical Narrative by   *Edward Merillat Moses*

EDWARD M. MOSES AND ROBERT A. GETZ, PUBLISHERS
ALEXANDRIA, VIRGINIA

REVISED EDITION

Copyright © 1995 by Edward M. Moses and Robert A. Getz, Publishers
P.O. Box 17331, Alexandria, Virginia 22302

All rights reserved. No part of this book may be reproduced
in any form or by any electronic, mechanical or other means
without the express written permission from the publisher.

The crest of the United States Military Academy is a registered trademark
of the United States of America and is used herein by permission of the
Superintendent of the United States Military Academy at West Point.

Cover design by Robert A. Getz
Book design by Edward M. Moses and Robert A. Getz, Publishers
Printed in the United States of America

Library of Congress Catalog Card Number 95-95174

ISBN 0-9648939-9-1

REVISED EDITION

DEDICATION

This book is dedicated to

THE UNITED STATES MILITARY ACADEMY

at West Point

and to her Sons and Daughters in the Long Gray Line.

May your ranks always be filled with America's finest and
"May our country in the hour of need be ready for the foe."

"E'er may that line of gray increase from day to day,
Live, serve, and die, we pray, West Point for thee."

ACKNOWLEDGEMENTS

I would like to acknowledge several persons and organizations for their valuable help in the development and completion of this book. First, I am indebted to my friends and associates at the Association of Graduates of the United States Military Academy, who were instrumental in the introduction of me and Ed Moses. Also, I want to thank Mrs. Judith Sibley in the Special Collections Department of the West Point Library for her generous assistance. Her interest and help were especially important in ensuring accuracy in the creation of many illustrations.

My sincere appreciation and thanks to an innovative and open-minded Ed Moses, who eloquently authored the narrative, while providing me with the opportunity to work creatively.

Finally, I want to express a very special thank you to my wife, Johnnie Lou, who kept my creativity alive and in perspective.

- Robert A. Getz
Illustrator

I wish to acknowledge certain individuals and organizations for helping to make this book possible. First, the staffs of several offices at the United States Military Academy and West Point were particularly helpful in providing requested information, including the Admissions Department, the Army Athletic Association, the Association of Graduates, and the West Point Museum. Also, the librarians and staff of the Alexandria Library System in Alexandria, Virginia, were always courteous and responsive and provided a great deal of reference material from the several libraries in that system. My thanks to Judy Lanier and Amelia Nickels Calhoun for their assistance in refining the text. I am of course greatly indebted to my illustrator, Robert A. Getz, who persevered in the creation of many more sketches than we had originally contemplated and who did so with a great sense of humor and commitment as we pushed ahead, page by page.

In 1951, retired Army Colonel R. Ernest Dupuy wrote an inspiring book entitled *Men of West Point*. Colonel Dupuy's book was by far my most valuable reference source. I used it extensively and I recommend it to anyone desiring to read more about West Point's graduates. Dr. Stephen B. Grove, USMA Historian at West Point, gave much of his valuable time on several occasions and made numerous suggestions and recommendations that were incorporated into the text. If there are any errors or omissions, they are mine.

I want also to acknowledge the not so obvious role of my parents, *Merillat Moses* (Class of 1931) and Grace McLean Moses. Their appreciation of West Point, as a bastion of values and a producer of role models, was shared so many times in conversations with this son. Also, my wife, Margaret Erskine Calhoun ("Frou"), contributed numerous valuable suggestions and hours helping to edit a narrative that was always competing for space with the many dramatic sketches. I am greatly indebted to her for her understanding and for being there when needed.

- Edward Merillat Moses
Author

INTRODUCTION

Rarely does a person have the opportunity to write about something that is really personally important, so when I was asked to write an historical sketchbook about the United States Military Academy at West Point, I readily accepted. Like most graduates, many of my values were shaped at that unique institution. Character and values are what West Point is all about, and most graduates learn this when they are cadets. Later in life, West Point's values are a continual source of pride and sustenance to members of *The Long Gray Line,* as each comes to acknowledge and to accept the vital importance of character to an individual, a leader, and a country.

It was first necessary to locate a skillful "pen and ink" artist - one capable of creating a wide range of drawings, while capturing the spirit of West Point. Fortunately, I was able to contact Robert A. Getz, a member of the Department of Geography and Environmental Engineering, who has done illustrative work for the Association of Graduates at West Point for many years. All of Bob Getz's "pen and ink" drawings are original and creatively illustrate the historical text.

In writing the narrative, I wanted it to be light and fast reading, reasonably concise and to highlight selected West Point graduates and their contributions to the nation. It's an amazing record in many fields of endeavor. Since the lasting value of an institution is best measured by the quality of its product over time, it was important to start in the beginning and to end in the present - almost two centuries. As the story unfolded, an important question arose: why has West Point been able to consistently produce *"leaders of high moral character for the nation"*? The answer gave birth to *The Making of Leaders,* sections of the book that highlight cadet life at West Point. Finally, and hopefully, I wanted the book to be of interest to both non-graduates and graduates, cadets and prospective cadets and their families and friends - a very wide audience.

As the book progressed, I discovered much about West Point and its graduates that I either never knew or had somehow forgotten over the years. Certainly, for every graduate included in this book there are literally hundreds of other graduates, who have pursued their life's work with the same excellence and dedication as those who have been more visible. I regret not having been able to include them as there are so many. Perhaps there will be another opportunity. However, I have tried to emphasize the breadth of graduate contributions in many different career fields - war and peace, science, education, exploration, industry, politics and statesmanship. Their remarkable accomplishments carry the message loud and clear that West Point and its graduates have strongly influenced the development of our nation. We hope that the reading of this book either establishes or reenforces that thought. We also hope that the reader understands that it is West Point's values that are supremely important to the nation and that graduate accomplishments are but the proof of the pudding. If young men and women who are contemplating a career in the service of their country find this book to be informative and of value, then we think we will have done something worthwhile. If cadets find that this book helps them to share West Point's values with their families and friends, then *The Long Gray Line* will rejoice in our mutual pride in those wonderful values. We hope that you, the reader, enjoy reading this very different historical sketchbook about West Point and her graduates as much as we enjoyed creating it.

- Edward Merillat Moses
Class of 1954, U.S.M.A.

WEST POINT

THE MAKING OF LEADERS

AN HISTORICAL SKETCH BOOK

- TABLE OF CONTENTS -

Acknowledgements	*iv*
Introduction	*v*
The Long Gray Line	11
The Father of the Military Academy	12
General George Washington	13
The Father of our Country	14
Polish Patriot	15
The Making of Leaders - The New Cadet	
"Beast Barracks"	16
Benny Havens' Tavern	17
The Seminole Indian War	18
The Mexican War	19
"Flying Artillery"	20
Scott's Fixed Opinion	21
The Making of Leaders - Military Leadership	
The "Whole Person" Leader	22
Yearling Summer	23
Firstie and Cow Summers	24
The Civil War	25
Lincoln's General	26
Battle Monument	27
Sedgwick Monument	28
The War in the West	29
Lee's Decision	30
"Stonewall" Falls	31
The Confederate "High Tide"	32,33
Surrender at Appomattox	34,35
Civil War "Firsts"	36
The Making of Leaders - Education	
Academic Excellence	37
Academic Facilities	38,39
Exploring the West	40
Railroad Pioneers	41
Industry and Science	42
Mapping the Nation	43
Educating the Nation	44

The American Indian Wars	45
Robert's Rules of Order	46

The Making of Leaders - Character
Honor and Discipline	47
Spiritual Growth	48
The Cadet Prayer	49
Heritage and Pride	50
Benny Havens, Oh!	51

The Spanish American War	52
Michie Stadium	53
Building the Panama Canal	54
The World at War	55
Pershing Barracks	56
Scientist George Squier	57

The Making of Leaders - Physical Training — 58
"Every Cadet an Athlete"	59
Intercollegiate Sports	60
Football at West Point	61
Army Blue	62

Preparing for World War II	63
War in the Pacific	64
Statesman - Philosopher	65
The "Great Crusade"	66
American Hero - President	67
"The Soldier's General" and His Warrior	68
Air Power's Role	69
Nuclear Engineer - Governor - Educator	70

The Making of Leaders - Extracurricular Activities
Eisenhower Hall and Cullum Hall	71
Delafield Pond	72
Cadet Recreation	73

The Association of Graduates	74
The Korean War	75
Advisors to Presidents	76
The Vietnam War	77
Space Age Pioneers	78
The Alma Mater	79
Desert Storm	80,81
Graduate Pathfinders	82,83

The Making of Leaders - Graduation
Graduation Week	84
The Corps	85
Graduation	86,87

Bibliography	88

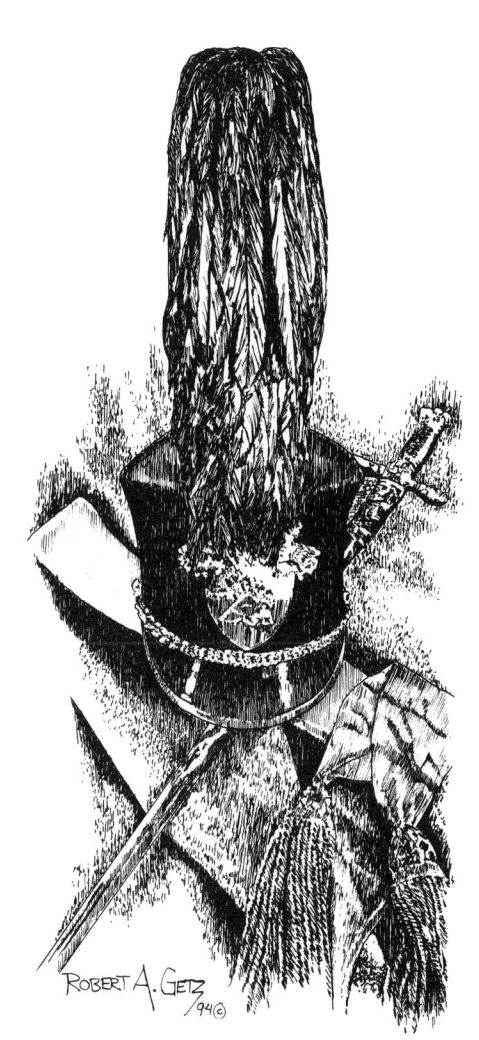

The Long Gray Line

Throughout history, great nations have established and nurtured institutions that have proved to be fundamental in assuring their acceptance as leaders among nations. Such an institution is the United States Military Academy at West Point, New York, which has a remarkable history of major contributions to America's greatness. Early advocates of the establishment of a military academy included Colonel Henry Knox, Alexander Hamilton and future presidents George Washington and John Adams. On March 16, 1802, President Thomas Jefferson signed into law the Act of Congress authorizing the Military Academy at West Point.

Many Americans are unaware of the important role played by West Point graduates in two centuries of national growth - during which time we progressed from exploring the West to exploring the Moon. The many valuable contributions of these graduates are rooted in the intellectual, leadership and character development training they received at the Military Academy. It is this training that has established West Point as a unique national institution.

When a graduate visualizes *The Long Gray Line* of the Corps of Cadets, the image has a special meaning for thousands of her sons and daughters. It represents a shared core of knowledge, character, code of conduct, and an understanding of the meaning of the Academy's motto - *Duty, Honor, Country*. It represents a bonding gained through the sharing of common experiences, learned self-discipline, and the knowledge that to lead one must first be led. It represents the knowledge that everyone will always do their duty to the best of their ability. *The Long Gray Line* is like a giant oak tree, tall and protective, its living leaves nourished by the fallen, with a deep tap root of American values - honorable and worthy of defending.

In 1817, Sylvanus Thayer (Class of 1808) was appointed Superintendent at West Point by President James Monroe, a post he held until 1833. Following distinguished service in the War of 1812, Thayer had been ordered to France to observe the operation of that country's military schools. The lessons he learned in France resulted in major military and academic reforms at West Point. In accomplishing these reforms, Thayer had the strong support of both Monroe and his Secretary of War, John C. Calhoun of South Carolina. Improved discipline and academic excellence were among his goals, and his reforms included mandatory study periods, small classes with cadets assigned according to their ability, and daily recitations in all subjects.

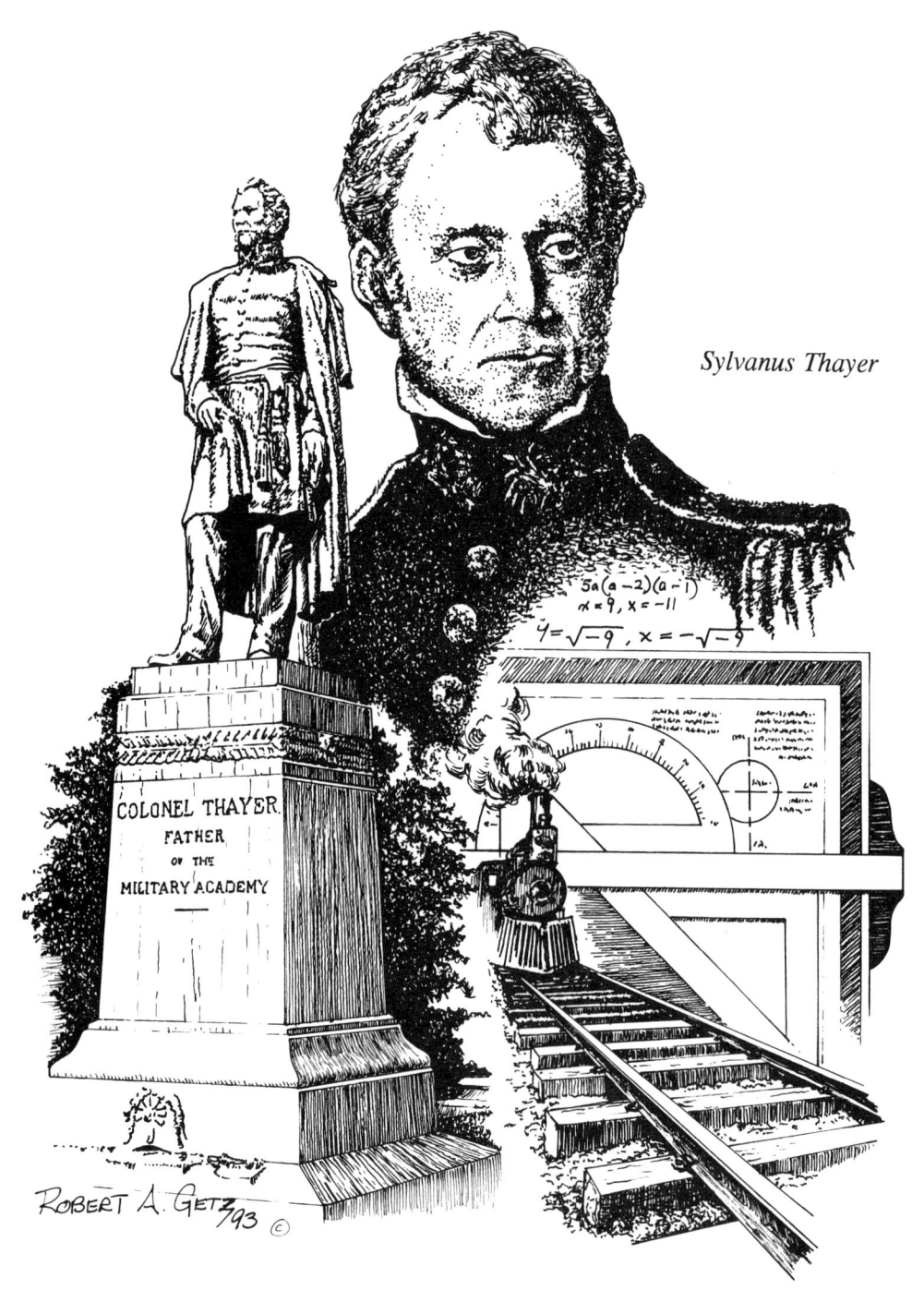

The Father of the Military Academy

The Military Academy was the *first* civil engineering school in America and a leading institution in the teaching of mathematics. For many years, its graduates "seeded" engineering and mathematics departments throughout the country. They were founders and presidents of other universities and chaired numerous academic departments. Graduates were directly responsible for the construction of major roads, railroads, bridges, buildings and canals. "Engineering" was synonymous with West Point graduates, who were in such great demand for civilian projects that Congress had to lengthen the mandatory service requirement after graduation. In recognition of his lasting achievements, graduates have gratefully acknowledged Sylvanus Thayer as *The Father of the Military Academy*. He *"ranks as one of the greatest educators our nation has produced."*

General George Washington

    During the Revolutionary War, George Washington recognized the strategic importance of West Point and the Hudson River. The river narrows at West Point with a sharp bend that facilitates the interdiction of river traffic. If the British, who occupied New York City to the south, controlled the Hudson River, the New England states would be separated from the rest of the country. Because the river was essential to both commerce and defense, Washington sent Colonel Thaddeus Kosciusko to West Point with orders to turn it into a fortified bastion.

    A national military academy was first suggested by Colonel Henry Knox in 1776. Colonel Knox served as General Washington's Chief of Artillery during the war, and later was appointed Secretary of War when Washington became president. Washington also supported a national military academy and favored its location at West Point. His recommendation was an important factor in the authorization and location of a military academy at West Point by the Congress.

Washington Monument

The Father of Our Country

The spirit of George Washington is an enduring part of the West Point experience. Gifted by an anonymous donor, Washington Monument was unveiled on May 20, 1916. It stands as a constant reminder of the values of "virtue" and "religion and morality" to the "political prosperity" of the nation that were so eloquently expressed in Washington's Farewell Address. Washington Monument is located on the Plain in front of Washington Hall - the 4,500 seat cadet dining hall. From there, the *Father of our Country* faces east toward the battlements of Fort Clinton and then further eastward to the Hudson River.

Polish Patriot

Kosciusko Monument

Colonel Thaddeus Kosciusko, professional soldier from Poland and Revolutionary War patriot, arrived at West Point in the Spring of 1778. General Washington had entrusted to him the construction of West Point's defenses. In two years, he completed a system of mutually supporting forts, redoubts and batteries that were acknowledged to be the strongest in America.

Prior to Kosciusko's arrival, a great chain had been forged at Sterling Iron Works, near West Point. It was 1,700 feet long, weighed over 186 tons and was anchored with bolts, stone and blocks of wood. One anchor was near Flirtation Walk on the west river bank; the other was on Constitution Island to the east. Kosciusko incorporated the chain into his overall defensive plan. Ft. Arnold, renamed Ft. Clinton following Benedict Arnold's treachery, was constructed near Trophy Point. Ft. Putnam was built to the west, above the Plain, where it's fields of fire overlooked both Ft. Clinton and the chain. Additional battery emplacements supported the two major forts and the southern approach was protected by three smaller redoubts.

In 1828, the Corps of Cadets honored the Polish patriot by erecting a monument on Ft. Clinton Parapet. In 1913, the Polish Clergy and Laity of the United States presented USMA with a statue of Kosciusko, which now rests atop the original monument. His sword is in the West Point Museum. It's inscribed, "Draw me not without reason; sheath me not without honor."

THE MAKING OF LEADERS

THE NEW CADET

"Beast Barracks"

Students at few educational institutions can match the well-rounded qualifications of new cadets entering the Military Academy. Their mean SAT scores are well above the national average for college-bound students. Candidates for admission must satisfy rigorous academic, medical and physical aptitude requirements, in order to gain entrance to the Military Academy. Over 85 percent of selected candidates rank in the top fifth of their class academically. Most have demonstrated a high potential for leadership through selection as class presidents or team captains and by participation in extracurricular activities such as varsity athletics and scouting. The New Cadet Class is exceptionally diverse and includes men and women from every state, race and religion in the nation. Over one-half of new cadets are nominated by members of the Congress and about one-fourth are nominated by the Secretary of the Army from a variety of categories that include enlisted members of the Regular Army, Reserves and National Guard.

In June, the New Cadet begins two months of Cadet Basic Training - "Beast Barracks." This intensive and rigorous training includes athletics, drill, marches, night bivouacs and basic weapon orientation. It ends in mid-August, when the Corps accepts the new Plebes at a parade ceremony marking the start of the new academic year. Jean-Jacques Rousseau once said, "The first thing a child should learn is how to endure. It is what he will have most need to know." Beast Barracks *is* endurance - an unforgettable common experience of *The Long Gray Line*!

Benny Havens, Jefferson Davis, Edgar Allan Poe and William T. Sherman (l. to r.)

Benny Havens' Tavern

Cadets had few opportunities for unobserved relaxation. Therefore, it was with great anticipation that they noted the new tavern that opened in Buttermilk Falls in 1824. The proprietor, Benny Havens, had returned to the area after an absence of several years. Over the next fifty years his tavern would acquire the "status of a West Point institution" and would be "honored by song, story and hundreds of cadet visitors" whose many escapades became legend. They were drawn there by "Benny's buckwheat cakes, oysters, or roast turkey washed down by a mug of hot flip" - a mix of beaten eggs, spices and ale. Regulars included cadets William T. Sherman, Edgar Allan Poe and Jefferson Davis. "Cump" Sherman, future Civil War general, loved Benny's oysters. Davis, future President of the Confederacy, was caught at the tavern, fled with the commandant in hot pursuit and fell off a cliff, breaking his arm and suffering internal injuries. Poe, American poet and creator of the detective story, referred to Benny Havens as "the only congenial soul in this God forsaken place." In 1838, a visiting Army doctor, Lt. Lucius O'Brien, memorialized the tavern and its proprietor with the initial verses of *Benny Havens, Oh!*, sung to the tune of *The Wearin o' the Green*.

The Seminole Indian War

Chief Osceola

Old Cadet Chapel

Dade Monument

Between 1817 and 1839 the nation fought to pacify the fiercely independent Seminole Indians in the Everglades of Florida. Their leader was Chief Osceola, "a half breed of great talents and audacity," who skillfully used the swamps as a sanctuary. On December 24, 1835, Major Francis L. Dade with 117 men marched from Ft. Brooke on Tampa Bay to reinforce Ft. King. Four days later he was ambushed by an overwhelming Seminole force in the Wahoo Swamp. Dade fell dead from the first shot - fired by Chief Micanopy as a signal to begin the ambush. The battle lasted five hours, with one survivor escaping. Among the dead were four graduates, including David Moniac (Class of 1822). A full-blooded Creek Indian, Moniac is recognized as the Military Academy's *first* Native American graduate. Osceola surrendered in the fall of 1837 and died while a prisoner. Zachary Taylor soon entered the Everglades with a large force that finally broke the Seminole's will to resist.

Dade Monument memorializes Dade, the soldiers of his command and *thirteen* graduates who lost their lives in the Seminole War. The monument is near the entrance to the post cemetery. In the background is the Old Cadet Chapel. Originally built in 1836 near the Clock Tower on the Plain, the chapel was relocated stone by stone to its present site in 1910.

As the Seminole War concluded, the nation was entering a period of rapid growth. Texas had won its independence from Mexico and was admitted as the 28th state on December 29, 1845. The stage was now set for the resolution of a boundary dispute with Mexico - the territory between the Nueces and Rio Grande Rivers. The first major battle was at Palo Alto on the Rio Grande River on May 8, 1846, where Zachary Taylor repulsed a Mexican force with heavy losses. The war with Mexico would soon demonstrate the value of a professional officer corps.

In March, 1847, Winfield Scott assumed command of the main force assembled to seize Mexico City. Against overwhelming numbers and extended lines of communication, Scott waged a brilliant campaign - winning every battle and skirmish. United States Military Academy graduates were a major factor in his success. Among those officers who distinguished themselves were Bliss, Bragg, Davis, Grant, Jackson, Johnston, Lee, McClellan, Meade, Porter, and Sherman. Most had studied under Professor Dennis Hart Mahan (Class of 1824), for whom Mahan Hall is named. Mahan was Thayer's protegé and was a recognized authority on the military arts. He preached "war of movement," "spirit of the offensive" and "the annihilation of the enemy's fighting power." His impact on graduates and the Army was best summarized by George W. Cullum (Class of 1833), memorialized by Cullum Hall, who said Mahan *"performed such an important part in the education of nearly our entire Army then living."*

The performance of West Point graduates in the Mexican War was exceptional. Zachary Taylor, soon to be our next President, referred to Albert Johnston (Class of 1826) as the "the best soldier I ever commanded." Winfield Scott called Robert E. Lee's (Class of 1829) reconnaissance at Contreras, after seven others had failed, "the greatest feat of physical and moral courage performed by any individual in my knowledge" and stated, "Lee is the greatest commander in America. In case of another war, his life should be insured for five million dollars." William Loring, soldier of fortune, when asked to relate the bravest act he had ever witnessed, replied, "Fitz-John Porter at the assault on the City of Mexico." Porter (Class of 1845), his soldiers dead or wounded, singlehandedly dragged a howitzer forward to within 100 yards of the enemy, stopped an infantry sortie and engaged the Mexican batteries. Jefferson Davis (Class of 1828), sorely wounded with a shattered heel and with his boot filled with blood, twice maneuvered his troops to repulse attacks at Buena Vista. Thomas J. Jackson (Class of 1846), first stood as a "stonewall" at Chapultepec. Isolated forward of his troops who had taken cover, he engaged the enemy infantry and artillery batteries with a single cannon. Standing in withering fire, he rallied his troops by shouting "There's no danger! See, I'm not hit!" Ordered to retire, he continued to hold his ground. George E. Pickett, Jackson's classmate, was among the first into Chapultepec, where he raised the Stars and Stripes over the city.

The imaginative employment of artillery was a major factor in Scott's success. Perhaps remembering Mahan's emphasis on "mobile warfare" and "speed," the artillery units commanded by graduates became known as "flying artillery." Artillerymen Samuel Ringgold (Class of 1818), killed at Palo Alto, James Duncan (Class of 1834), Braxton Bragg (Class of 1837) and Randolph Ridgely (Class of 1837) played important roles in determining the outcome of many battles. Mounted on the interior walls of the Administration Building foyer at West Point are two six-pounder guns, captured by the Mexicans when a battery commanded by John P. J. O'Brien (Class of 1836) was overrun. Recaptured by Simon Drum (Class of 1830), they bear the inscription "Lost without dishonor at the battle of Buena Vista by a Company of the 4th Artillery. Re-captured with just pride and exultation by the same regiment at Contreras."

Scott's Fixed Opinion

"I give it as my fixed opinion, that but for our graduated cadets, the war between the United States and Mexico might, and probably would have lasted some four or five years, with, in its first half, more defeats than victories falling to our share; whereas, in less than two campaigns, we conquered a great country and a peace without the loss of a single battle or skirmish."

- *General Winfield Scott*

There were 523 graduates in Scott's army. Of these, 447 won battlefield promotions for distinguished service. At a victory dinner in December, 1847, Scott toasted West Point. "*But for its science, this army multiplied by four could not have entered the capital of Mexico.*" On February 2, 1848, a treaty was concluded with Mexico that formally ceded to the United States the disputed Texas territory to the Rio Grande River, New Mexico and Upper California.

THE MAKING OF LEADERS

MILITARY LEADERSHIP

The "Whole Person" Leader

"*The purpose of the United States Military Academy is to provide the Nation with leaders of character who serve the common defense.*" West Point develops a "whole person" leader by encouraging "personality in leadership." The essence of leadership is the successful resolution of problems. Graduates have always been recognized as "doers" and "problem solvers," while demonstrating wide differences in personality. The total immersion of cadets at West Point ensures that the common "shaping" experiences are derived from their academic, military, physical and moral training, while supporting the Academy's "whole person" leadership concept.

The Corps of Cadets lives in a continuous leadership development environment. Classroom instruction; chain of command, instructor and troop assignments; and the development of personal soldier skills produce a confident cadet leader. This leader is highly educated, self-disciplined, competitive and a true believer in Douglas MacArthur's (Class of 1903) enduring message, "*From the Far East, I send you one single thought... there is no substitute for victory.*"

MILITARY LEADERSHIP

Yearling Summer

After completing Cadet Basic Training in Beast Barracks during the first summer, the Yearling Third Class spend their second summer in Cadet Field Training at Camp Buckner, located on Lake Popolopen at the western edge of the Reservation. The camp is named for Simon Bolivar Buckner (Class of 1908), a former Commandant of Cadets. Buckner was killed on Okinawa in World War II, while leading the Tenth Army. Training for the Yearling cadets emphasizes the development of crew, squad and platoon level skills with "hands-on" equipment familiarization. It includes training in all of the combat arms - armor, infantry, field artillery and engineers - as well as battlefield communications. The Yearlings also conduct Maneuver Heavy Training as part of an armor and mechanized infantry Combined Arms Team. Third Class Cadet Field Training is led by selected First Class cadets, "Firsties", assisted by "Cow" Second Class cadets.

MILITARY LEADERSHIP

Firstie and Cow Summers

Summer training for the First and Second Classes, seniors and juniors, consists of a combination of leadership activities conducted worldwide. At West Point, cadets of both classes spend a part of one summer as leader-instructors with either the Fourth Class Cadet Basic Training or the Third Class Cadet Field Training programs. During these two summers, they are also assigned to either a tour as a Drill Cadet Leader at a U.S. Army training center or to Cadet Troop Leader Training at an Army post in the United States or overseas. Cadets of both classes participate in Individual Advanced Development assignments that may include Airborne, Air Assault, Survival or Mountain Warfare training at Army posts in the United States. These leadership and training assignments develop a high level of individual confidence and self-esteem.

Over 600,000 were to die as two very different societies, the industrial North and the agrarian South, fought a *total war* more violent than any the world had ever witnessed. The issues and causes were complex: a strong central government versus states rights, first advocated by South Carolina thirty years earlier; tariffs that favored industry over farming; slavery in the South, where 88 percent of the world's cotton was produced with the cotton gin; poor communication, encouraged by east-west railroads and westward migration; the publication of prejudicial sectional books; and demagogues who influenced public opinion. Bitter arguments raged for thirty years following the abandonment of slavery in the North. They also raged at West Point, where cadets had to make painful decisions as to where their true loyalties lay.

On December 20, 1860, South Carolina seceded from the Union, followed over the next three months by Mississippi, Florida, Alabama, Georgia, Louisiana and Texas. At dawn on April 12, 1861, P.G.T. Beauregard (Class of 1838) ordered the bombardment of Ft. Sumter in Charleston harbor and Wade Hampton Gibbes (Class of 1860) fired the first shell at Robert Anderson's (Class of 1825) defending force. The die was cast and graduates were at the forefront on each side. Virginia soon left the Union, followed by Arkansas, Tennessee and North Carolina.

Families were suddenly rent apart - brother against brother, friend against friend and cadet against cadet. At West Point, there were 278 cadets, including 86 southern cadets - 65 resigned and joined the South. No graduate was then a general officer in the Army. Soon, 294 would become Union generals and 151 would become Confederate generals. Many quickly became household names, including Grant, Sedgwick, Sheridan, Sherman, Thomas and Wilson for the Union and Ewell, Hill, Hood, Jackson, Johnston, Longstreet, Stuart and Pickett for the Confederacy.

The South called it the War Between the States and the North called it the Civil War. The North had overwhelming resources - three times the fighting population; twice the railroad mileage; five times the factories; ten times the workers; and ten times the value of products. Yet the war lasted four bloody years with the sheer weight of numbers finally overcoming southern esprit and superior leadership. At the end it was Ulysses S. Grant (Class of 1843) grinding away in a war of attrition against Robert E. Lee (Class of 1829) - maneuvering as in a chess game. And then Lee, his army stripped of muscle, tired, hungry, poorly equipped and in retreat, met with Grant at Appomattox Court House under a white flag. There, in the McLean House, it was time for the renewal of old cadet and army friendships, exchanging family news and grieving for lost comrades. They had all done their duty and could now go home.

Abraham Lincoln

Ulysses S. Grant

Lincoln's General

The personalities in the war dominate its history. Grant, who had left the army, returned by taking command of an Illinois volunteer regiment. Withdrawn, he smoked cigars and whittled constantly. His reputation was made in the West at Forts Henry and Donelson and later at Vicksburg, where with "audacity, vision and strategical ability," he abandoned his resupply lines and defeated J. Pemberton (Class of 1837), while Joseph Johnston (Class of 1829) was contained. His single-mindedness was demonstrated when a division commander telegraphed him, "Do you realize that if I advance my division will be wiped out?" Grant replied, "I am glad you understand your orders." Grant applied Mahan's *total war* concept taught at USMA, when he ordered Sherman (Class of 1840) to "*get into the interior of the enemy's country as far as you can, inflicting all the damage you can against their war resources....*" President Lincoln, under pressure to relieve Grant after he had sustained heavy casualties, said, "I can't do without this man. He fights." Lee, who relied greatly on insights into the personalities of Union commanders, was soliciting such information one evening around a campfire. R.E. "Dick" Ewell (Class of 1840), a corps commander, responded, "There is one West Pointer, I think in Missouri, and I hope the Northerners won't find out about him. I mean Sam Grant. He was at West Point with me when I was a cadet. He's clear-headed, quick and daring." Despite his apparent detachment, Grant could also show feelings. Upon the death of James B. McPherson (Class of 1853), killed by a bullet in the heart while rallying his troops, Grant said, "The country has lost one of its best soldiers - and I have lost my best friend." He grieved for hours, alone in his tent. After Lee's surrender at Appomattox Court House, he said, "What General Lee's feelings were, I do not know...but my own feelings...were sad and depressed." In 1869, Grant was elected to the first of two terms as President of the United States. He is entombed in New York City.

Battle Monument

Late in the war, a group of disabled teachers at West Point were concerned that the Regular Army's contribution to the war was not being adequately recognized, because the Union Army consisted mainly of volunteer regiments from the states. A committee of these disabled officers began to solicit private donations from army friends and comrades for a Regular Army memorial. Over many years they raised $60,000 and began construction of the memorial in 1889.

Located on Trophy Point, Battle Monument was dedicated on May 31, 1897. It is a memorial to the officers and soldiers of the Regular Army killed in the Civil War. The statue *Victory* stands atop the *largest* polished granite shaft in the Western Hemisphere. There are 2,230 names inscribed on this majestic monument that overlooks the scenic Hudson River Valley.

John Sedgwick

Joseph Hooker

Sedgwick Monument

John Sedgwick (Class of 1837), led the Union VI Corps in 1863 and 1864. At Chancellorsville, where his classmate Joseph Hooker commanded the Union Army, he conducted a surprise diversionary night crossing of the Rappahannock River at Fredericksburg. Four days later, to relieve pressure on Hooker, he assaulted and seized Mayre's Heights, strongly defended by his classmate Jubal Early. In May, 1864, his VI Corps held firm against a strong Confederate attempt to turn Grant's flank in the Wilderness. Three days later, at Spotsylvania Court House, the two armies met again as Lee maneuvered to block Grant's southern movement toward Richmond. From hastily erected breastworks, snipers harassed the Union troops for two days. While reassuring his men, Sedgwick shouted, "...they can't hit an elephant at that distance!" At that instant, the popular commander fell dead with a sniper's bullet in his brain. Grant, who had been with Sedgwick only five minutes earlier, numbly said, "So he's really dead? So he's really dead?" Lee also mourned his and his wife's "dear old friend," Major Sedgwick of the old "Army Blue" days.

Sedgwick Monument is a memorial from the soldiers of the VI Corps. Completed in 1868, it was cast from Confederate cannons captured by the VI Corps. Across the street from Battle Monument, it also overlooks the Hudson River- a familiar view to *Cadet* John Sedgwick.

The War in the West

William T. Sherman

George H. Thomas

William T. Sherman (Class of 1840) fought in the west with Grant. When Grant went east to oppose Lee, Sherman remained as commander of the western forces. Two of Sherman's subordinates were George H. Thomas, his classmate and best friend at West Point, and James H. Wilson (Class of 1860). Thomas' decision to stay with the Union had resulted in the confiscation of his property in Virginia and banishment by his sisters, who never again spoke his name. In 1862, Thomas won the North's first victory at Mill Spring, Kentucky, where he smashed a Confederate force under George B. Crittenden (Class of 1832). At Chicamauga, a Union defeat, he rallied fleeing troops around his own men, acquiring the nickname "*the rock of Chicamauga.*" It is possible that, "*Thomas' stand...saved the Union Army in the West...and perhaps the war.*" Later, this same army under different leadership, Grant and then Sherman, would take Vicksburg and then march through Georgia, splitting the South. James Wilson practiced blitzkrieg warfare in March, 1865, with a cavalry penetration followed by a rapid exploitation deep behind enemy lines to seize the important Confederate supply depot at Selma, Alabama. Wilson then swept through Georgia, continued onward through South Carolina and finally linked up with Sherman in North Carolina. On May 11th, he captured Jefferson Davis, the fleeing Confederate president.

Jefferson Davis, Robert E. Lee, "Stonewall" Jackson (l. to r.)

Lee's Decision

In all of America, Robert E. Lee (Class of 1829) was widely recognized as the finest professional soldier in uniform. In March, 1861, Winfield Scott had offered Lee command of the Union Army and promotion to Major General. When Virginia subsequently seceded from the Union, Lee declined Scott's offer. Scott said, "Lee, you have made the greatest mistake of your life, but I feared you would do so." Lee submitted a one sentence letter of resignation from the Union Army: *"Save in defense of my native state, I never desire again to draw my sword."*

Lee accepted a Confederate commission and was soon serving as military advisor to Jefferson Davis (Class of 1828), President of the Confederate States of America. In June, 1862, Lee assumed command of the Confederate army then opposing George B. McClellan (Class of 1846) on the Peninsula and renamed it - the Army of Northern Virginia. Earlier, he had sent Thomas "Stonewall" Jackson (Class of 1846) rampaging through the Shenandoah Valley in a diversionary attack that was *"the most brilliant campaign in history."* He now recalled Jackson and in a series of battles at Mechanicsville, Gaines Mill and Malvern Hills, ended the Union threat to Richmond. Superior leadership had overcome a far larger and better equipped force. It was the beginning of a string of successes that would leave the Union reeling.

"Stonewall" Jackson

Robert E. Lee

"Stonewall" Falls

In 1863, Lee faced Joseph Hooker (Class of 1837) at Chancellorsville. He split his smaller force, sending Jackson on a concealed march around Hooker's right flank. There, Jackson shattered the XI Army Corps commanded by O. O. Howard (Class of 1854). In navy parlance, Jackson had crossed Hooker's "T". The Battle of Chancellorsville was effectively over - won *"against long odds by exploitation of the enemy's weakness and wholesale breakage of all the rules of war."* But Jackson was mortally wounded, shot by his own troops as he returned in fading light from a reconnaissance. His left arm shattered and amputated, he died a week later. Lee wept, saying, "I have lost my right arm." Later, historians would speculate that the outcome at Gettysburg, "the high tide of the Confederacy," might well have been different had Jackson been present. Lee's Chancellorsville victory is recorded as *"one of the world's military masterpieces."* In Lincoln's words, "it is horrible...one hundred and thirty thousand magnificent soldiers cut to pieces by less than sixty thousand ragamuffins." As Lee moved north toward Gettysburg, George G. Meade (Class of 1835) took command of the Union forces.

The Confederate "High Tide"

    Gettysburg was a meeting engagement of two armies. They met on July 1, 1863 and fought for three violent, bloody days. The Union Army held the high ground, as Lee struck both Union flanks and then the center. On the third day, James Longstreet's (Class of 1842) corps with George E. Pickett's (Class of 1846) division assaulted the Union center at Cemetery Ridge - 15,000 fresh troops supported by a two hour artillery bombardment from 150 cannons. The noise was "strange and terrible, a sound that came from thousands of throats…like a vast mournful roar," as Pickett's men crossed almost a mile of open fields. Only about 100 managed to penetrate the Union center. A distraught Pickett said to Longstreet, "General, I am ruined. My division is destroyed." Lee said to his commanders after the battle, "It is I who have lost this fight. You must help me out of it the best way you can." That night, a tired Lee mused, "I never saw troops behave more magnificently. Too bad! Too bad! Too bad!"

Surrender at Appomattox

The war continued for two years after Gettysburg, but the threat of Confederate offensive action in the north had passed. After Gettysburg, Lee nurtured his army, blocked, held and struck only when presented with an opportunity. He had acquired the nickname "The King of Spades" during the Peninsula campaign, because of his expertise in erecting field fortifications. This strength now stood the Army of Northern Virginia in good stead. Finally, in the spring of 1865, Lee was forced out of his fortified positions at Petersburg. He attempted a withdrawal to link up with remnants of Joseph E. Johnston's (Class of 1829) army in the western mountains of Virginia. Ignoring Richmond, Grant sought the complete destruction of Lee's army with an aggressive pursuit. Philip H. Sheridan's (Class of 1853) cavalry repeatedly struck Lee's flanks as he retreated, finally cutting off Lee's force at Appomattox Court House. While discussing surrender with his commanders, Lee said, "General Grant will not demand unconditional surrender; he will give us as honorable terms as we have a right to ask or expect." His insight into Grant was correct. George Meade, the Union commander at Gettysburg, visited with Lee the day after the surrender in McLean House. Lee asked, "What are you doing with all that gray in your beard?" Meade replied, "You have to answer for most of it." Another friendship came full circle in Richmond when President Lincoln visited the home of George Pickett and introduced himself as "George's old friend." Lincoln had corresponded with Pickett for years. As a young Congressman from Illinois, he had appointed the Virginian to the United States Military Academy. In September, 1865, Lee became President of Washington College in Lexington, later renamed Washington and Lee University. As he lay dying five years later, his thoughts on his gray-clad soldiers, he ordered, *Strike the tent!* - and joined them forever.

McLean House

Ulysses S. Grant

Robert E Lee

The war produced several *firsts* in new technologies and tactics. Herman Haupt (Class of 1835), Chief of Construction and Transportation of U.S. Military Railroads, had a prominent role in the first use of railroads to move troops and supplies. The importance of moving large troop formations by rail was demonstrated when Hooker's Corps moved from Virginia to Stevenson, Alabama, in seven days - 1,192 miles. The telegraph was used extensively for battlefield communication between major commanders and lines were frequently laid by advancing frontline troops. Sherman deployed topographical engineers forward of his troops to keep him advised of the terrain, roads and bridges. Gabriel J. Rains (Class of 1827) first employed minefields and booby traps to slow McClellan's advance on the Peninsula. This "most murderous and barbarous thing" was soon discontinued.

Henry L. Abbott (Class of 1854) manned balloons for aerial observation of the Confederate positions on the Peninsula. New cavalry tactics evolved, centered on the use of repeating carbines and pistols. Sheridan fine-tuned these new tactics into a form of fire and maneuver that was a precursor of future armored warfare, as his cavalry fought dismounted and then moved rapidly to strike again. Grant conducted the first combined arms amphibious operation with Flag Officer Foote on the Mississippi River during the Forts Henry and Donelson campaign. Battlefield mobility was taken to new heights by Jackson in the Shenandoah Valley Campaign, when his foot cavalry marched 400 miles, fought four battles on chosen terrain and defeated four different Union commanders in ten days.

Civil War "Firsts"

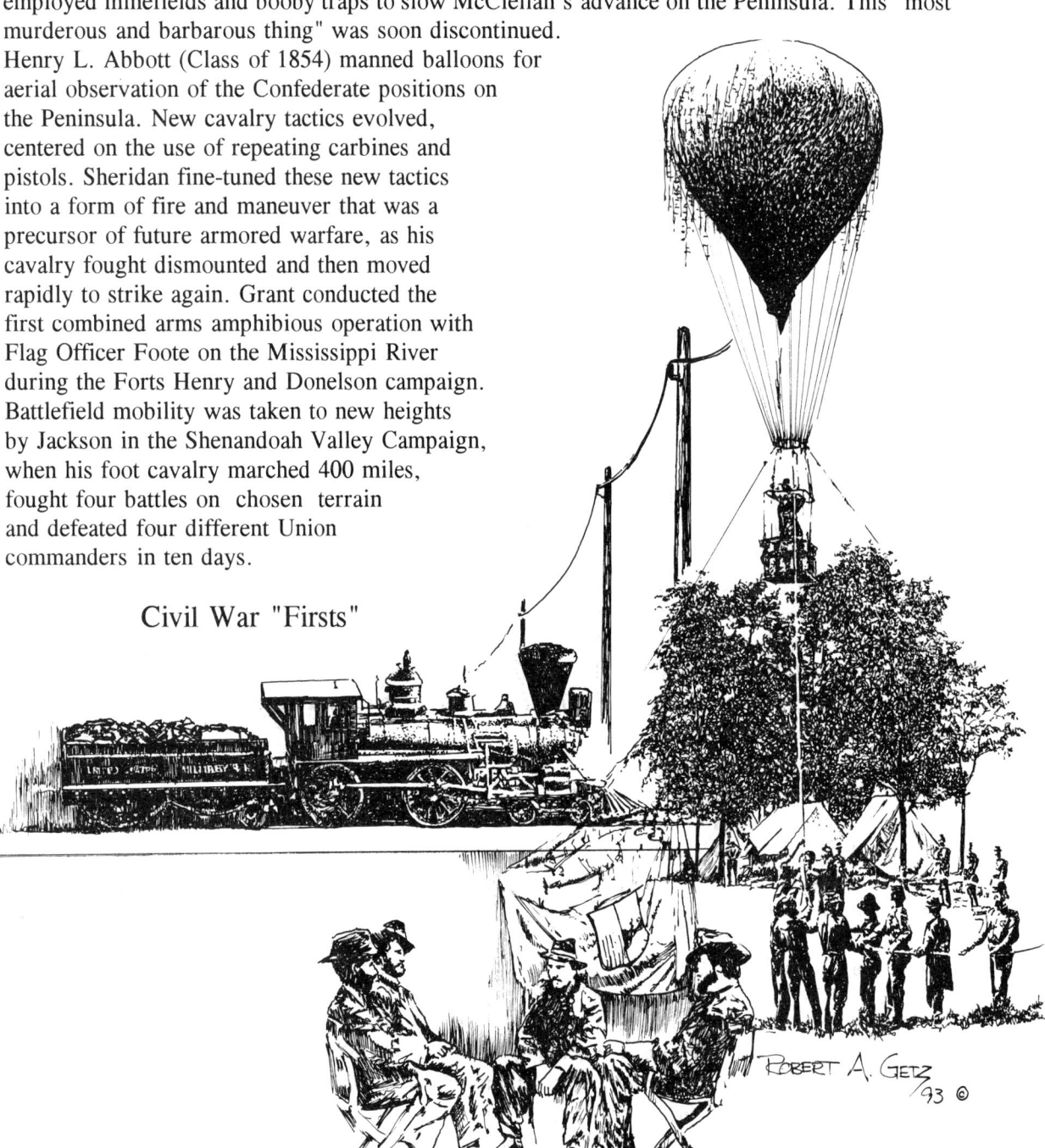

THE MAKING OF LEADERS

EDUCATION

Dennis H. Mahan

Mahan Hall

Academic Excellence

"*Graduates must be enlightened leaders... whose minds are creative, critical and resourceful.*" This academic philosophy has produced a broad arts and sciences curriculum supporting many different fields of study and majors programs, including civil, electrical, mechanical, nuclear and management engineering; economics; political science; behavioral science; history; and geography. A Summer Enrichment Program offers opportunities such as immersion language training, intern positions in federal agencies and study at other military and civilian educational institutions.

All First Class cadets take the Graduate Record Examination. Historically, the results have been impressive. In 1948, when the senior class was first tested on the General Education Test with a control group of seniors from 41 liberal arts colleges, the *average* cadet placed at the 72nd percentile. Most cadets who remain in the Army attend a fully funded masters program or some other scholarship or fellowship program. The United States Military Academy is the only institution in the nation that ranks in the top four in *both* Rhodes Scholarships and Hertz Foundation Fellowships. Graduates have also been awarded numerous National Science Foundation Fellowships and Marshall Scholarships.

The legacy of academic excellence dating back to Dennis H. Mahan (Class of 1824) - *first* in his class and a protegé of Sylvanus Thayer - survives today in a progressive curriculum producing enlightened military leaders. Mahan Hall, located on Thayer Road, is a nine story granite academic building with a 600 seat auditorium, modern classrooms and laboratories.

EDUCATION

Academic Facilities

The Military Academy academic facilities are among the finest in the world. The main academic buildings - Bartlett Hall, Lincoln Hall, Mahan Hall, Thayer Hall and Washington Hall - contain many modern classrooms for the personalized instruction of 15-20 cadets, well-equipped laboratories and several large auditoriums for departmental and guest speaker presentations. Closed circuit television and the latest scientific equipment and technology are available. Cadets and the faculty conduct operations research and analysis at the Operations Research Cell and basic and applied laser technology research at the Photonics Research Center. The use of computers is emphasized in academic studies and all cadets have their own high performance personal computer. A mainframe computer center provides an advanced time-sharing network, and a super minicomputer network offers file sharing, electronic mail, bulletin boards and printer access services.

A new four story granite library was completed in 1964 on the site of the old library. It has eight reference levels organized by subject. The library seats 800 cadets, is equipped with the latest in audio-visual and microfilm equipment and has a computerized library reference system. More than 500,000 books and 2,200 current periodicals occupy over 100,000 square feet of useable floor space. The numerous collections of the library include many rare books, maps and manuscripts; the personal papers of Omar N. Bradley (Class of 1915); and a collection of William Faulkner's first editions. A chronological pictorial overview of American history is engraved on three large bronze plaques located at the main entrance to the library.

Randolph Marcy, Benjamin Bonneville, Phillip Cooke (l. to r.)

Exploring the West

During the nineteenth century the nation expanded westward and established an industrial base that was to become the envy of the civilized world. Graduates played important roles in exploration, survey and mapping, transportation, industry, science and technology, education and politics. Randolph B. Marcy (Class of 1832) was posted in the West following graduation. His observations of ill-prepared settlers, wagon trains subjected to unanticipated hardships and Indian attacks caused him to write *The Praerie Traveller*, which he based on interviews with well known and experienced frontiersmen. Marcy's book became the "pioneer's bible" on how to organize, what to take and how to defend oneself on the long trek west. Later, Marcy surveyed routes over the Rockies that were heavily travelled during the 1849 Gold Rush. In 1830, Benjamin Bonneville (Class of 1815) organized an expedition that explored the Great Salt Lake, crossed the Sierras, found the headwaters of the Yellowstone, navigated the Columbia River and discovered the Humboldt River. His maps of the territory west of the Rockies *"lifted the curtain on the natural resources of the great West."* In 1832, James Allen (Class of 1829) entered the Minnesota wilderness on a 2,800 mile exploration of the headwaters of the Mississippi River, the St. Croix River and Lake Superior. Two years later, he submitted his report and valuable maps to the Secretary of War. Phillip Cooke (Class of 1827) opened an important southern route west for settlers between Sante Fe and San Diego, while leading a Mormon infantry battalion and General Kearney's wagon trains westward to California during the Mexican War.

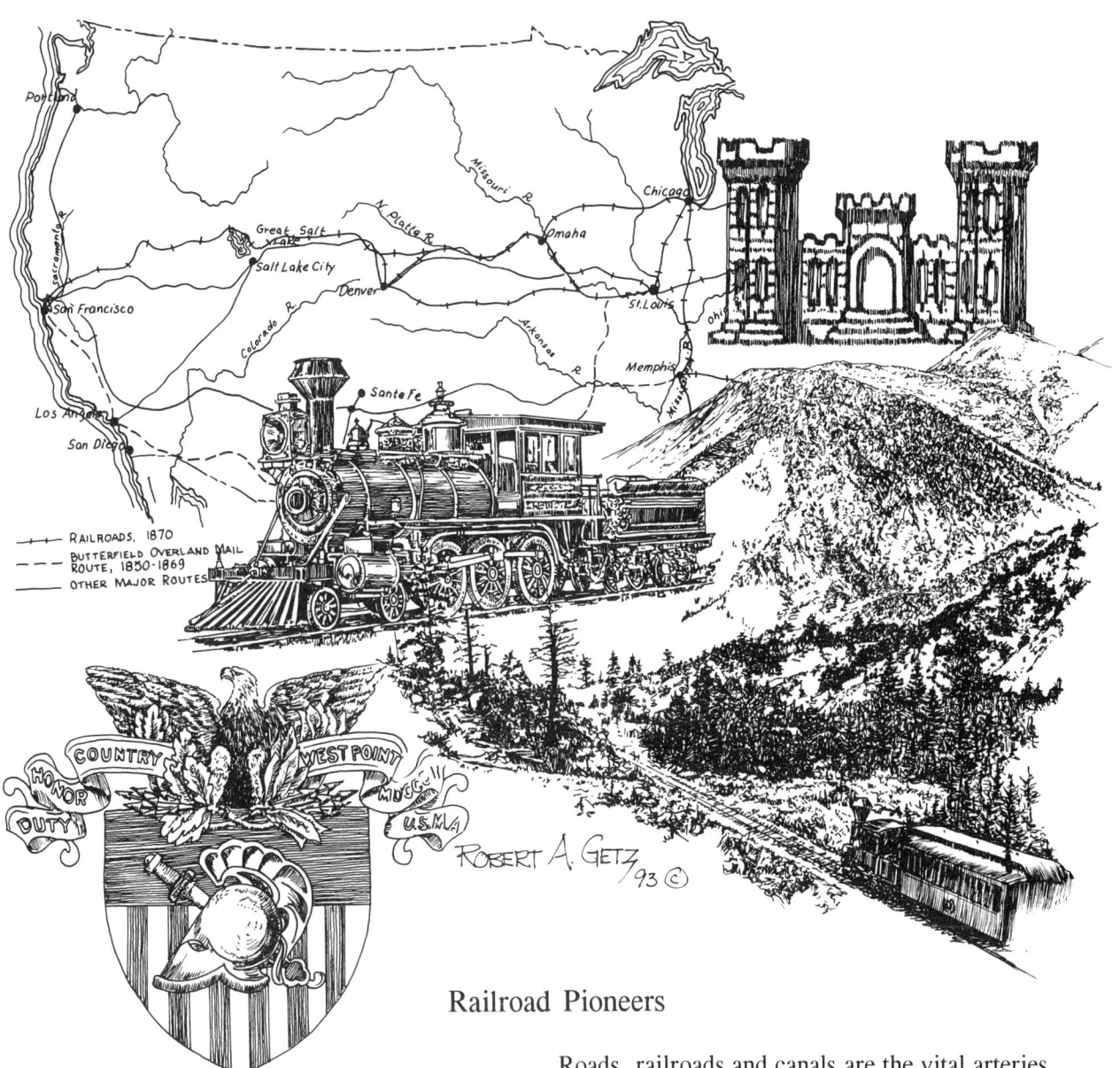

Railroad Pioneers

Roads, railroads and canals are the vital arteries of a nation and railroads were of particular importance in America. By 1900, twenty-two Military Academy graduates had become presidents of railroad companies, and about sixty had served as chief engineers of railroad companies. As author R. Ernest Dupuy noted, *"It would be hard to find a railroad in the United States which does not owe its original construction, at least in part, to the touch of the Long Gray Line."* In 1823, Congress directed the Corps of Engineers to perform surveys for roads and bridges. Thirty years later it authorized surveys for the development of a transcontinental railway from Mississippi to the Pacific Ocean. Graduate-led survey teams fought Indians, crossed endless prairies and mountains and endured untold hardships as they mapped the continent. In 1860, a railhead met Alexander Center's (Class of 1827) Overland Mail at Memphis, Tennessee.

Early graduate railroad pioneers included William McNeill (Class of 1817), George Whistler (Class of 1819), Joshua Barney (Class of 1820), Isaac Trimble, William Cook and Walter Gwynn (1822 Classmates), and John Dillahunty and R. Edward Hazzard (1824 Classmates). These graduates were the *first* recognized group of railroad engineers in America. Whistler engineered numerous improvements in the steam locomotive and invented the locomotive "whistle." In 1842, he began to build the Czar's St. Petersburg-Moscow Railroad. Whistler died there in 1849, and the Russian railroad was completed by Thompson Brown (Class of 1825).

Industry and Science

Henry Dupont

    Industry and science grew as America's transportation network expanded. In 1816, the Cold Spring Foundry was built opposite West Point by a group that included Joseph G. Swift (Class of 1802), the *first* USMA graduate. It was frequently called the West Point Foundry and in 1830 it produced *Best Friend*, America's *first* practical steam-driven locomotive. The foundry made castings for the Erie Canal, piping for the Croton aqueduct and the water pipes for Boston, Chicago and New York. Thomas J. Rodman's (Class of 1841) hollow casting and water cooling systems were perfected at the foundry. The steam engines for America's second steam frigate, *USS Fulton the Second*, and for the *USS Merrimac* were built at the Cold Spring Foundry.

    In 1834, Henry DuPont (Class of 1833) joined his father's powder mill and later ran the company as the family empire began to grow. DuPont's collaboration with Rodman on the production of gunpowder resulted in numerous improvements. His son, Henry A. DuPont (Class of 1861), served in the Civil War and assumed administrative control of the company in 1875.

    Several graduates were prominent in astronomy. Andrew Talcott (Class of 1818) invented the zenith telescope in 1834 and used it to determine latitude. In 1855, Ormsby M. Mitchel (Class of 1829) built an observatory with a 12 inch telescope, huge for that time, and invented the declinometer. In 1859, he was appointed superintendent of the largest observatory in America, the Dudley Observatory, and was elected a Fellow of the Royal Astronomical Society of London in 1861. Edward Holden (Class of 1870) became President of the University of California in 1885, and planned, designed and built the Lick Observatory with a 36 inch refracting telescope. He was its director for ten years and was also invited to join the Royal Astronomical Society. Holden was the *second* American to be awarded the coveted Danish Cross of Dannebrog "for services in the general field of science."

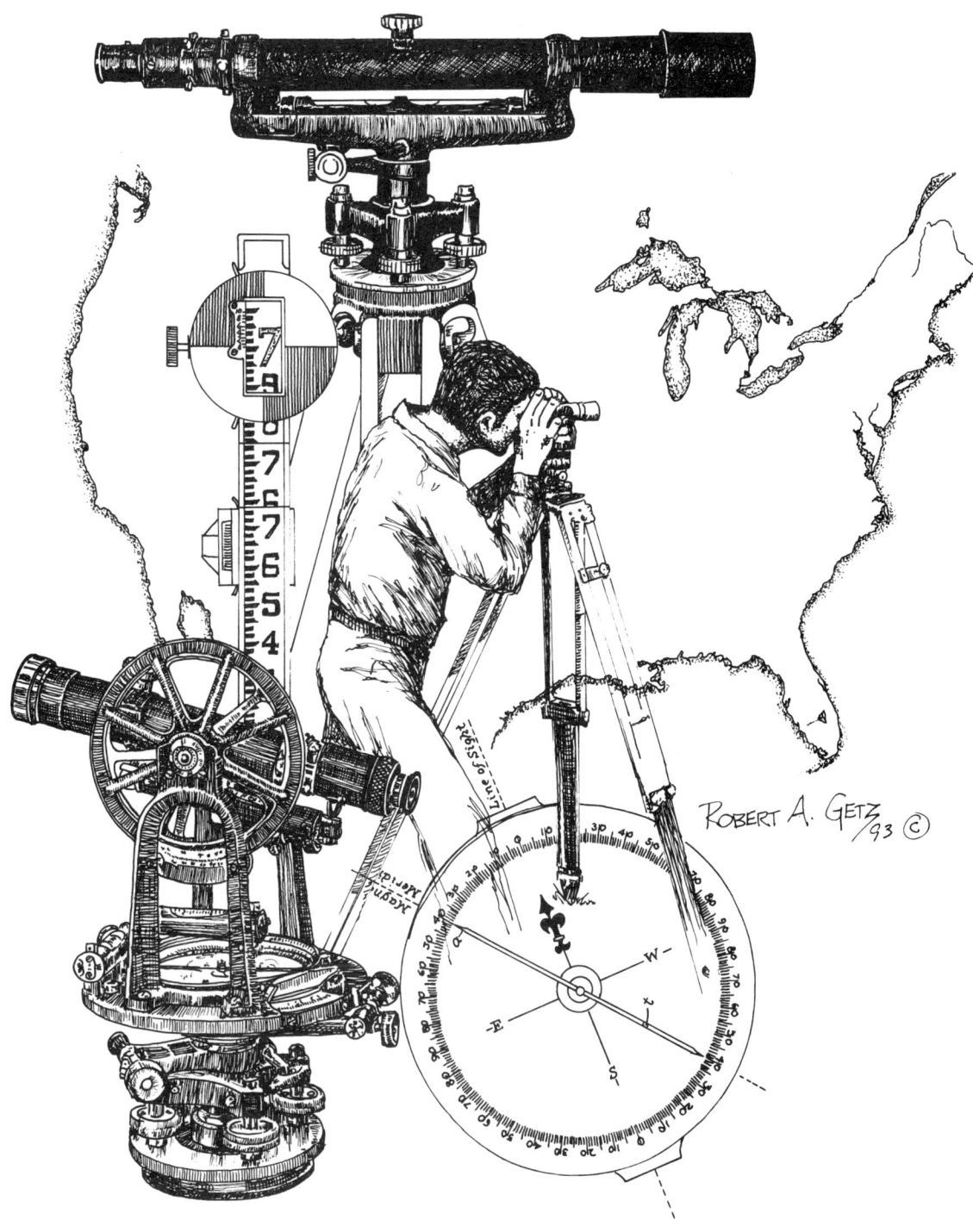

Mapping the Nation

The *first* American to be awarded the Danish Cross of Dannebrog was Alexander D. Bache (Class of 1825), great grandson of Benjamin Franklin. Bache was appointed director of the U.S. Coast and Geodetic Survey in 1843, following his selection by "the leading scientific and literary institutions." Bache surveyed and produced accurate charts along America's *entire* coastline - a truly monumental achievement! He also established the astronomically derived triangulation points that were then used as reference points for the survey and mapping of the *entire* continental United States. Bache also devised America's standard weights and measures systems. In 1846, he helped to found the Smithsonian Institute and he then *founded* the National Academy of Science in 1863. Bache was also a member of numerous other societies.

William H.C. Bartlett

Educating the Nation

Before 1840, "engineering was offered almost exclusively" at USMA. Harvard's Lawrence School of Engineering was founded in 1846 by Henry L. Eustis (Class of 1842), who served as professor and dean for 34 years. Yale's Sheffield School of Engineering was founded in 1847 and William A. Norton (Class of 1831) was appointed head of Civil Engineering, where he served for 31 years. In 1852, the University of Michigan founded its Engineering Department with William G. Peck (Class of 1844) directing both Physics and Civil Engineering.

Many graduates published important cornerstone textbooks. The list includes Charles Davies (Class of 1815), "one of the great mathematicians of the nineteenth century," who wrote *Surveying* and *Shades, Shadows and Perspective*. Davies also translated and revised *Bourdon's Algebra* and *Legendre's Geometry and Trigonometry*. Dennis H. Mahan (Class of 1824) wrote *Civil Engineering* and *Industrial Drawing*. William H.C. Bartlett (Class of 1826), for whom Bartlett Hall is named, wrote *Acoustics and Optics* and *Analytical Mechanics* and was a department head for 35 years. Bartlett was one of America's foremost astronomers and the *first* to use photography for astronomical measurements in America. He also helped to incorporate the National Academy of Science. Albert E. Church (Class of 1828) wrote *Calculus* and *Analytical Geometry* and historian Cadmus Wilcox's (Class of 1846) *Mexican War* history stood as "the definitive work" for decades.

Graduates *founded* several institutions of higher education. In 1839, Francis H. Smith (Class of 1833) was invited to organize and become the first superintendent of Virginia Military Institute. In 1835, Alden Partridge (Class of 1806) reestablished Norwich University in Vermont and became its President. Oliver O. Howard (Class of 1854) founded Howard University in Washington D.C. and Leonidas Polk (Class of 1827), the "Fighting Bishop," founded the University of the South at Sewanee.

United States Military Academy graduates have been presidents, superintendents and chancellors of many well known educational institutions. The list includes the Air Force Academy, the Citadel, the Universities of Alabama, Arkansas, Arkansas Industrial, California, Columbia, Lehigh, Louisiana, South Carolina and Washington and Lee, as well as Gonzaga, Hamilton College, Kenyon College and College of City of New York - an impressive testimonial to West Point's leadership contribution to American education!

*George A. Custer,
George Crook,
Charles King* (l.to r.)

The American Indian Wars

From 1790 to 1898 the Army fought 19 Indian wars and 69 campaigns. For years American Indians were taken advantage of by "carpetbaggers", who withheld treaty supplies while selling whiskey and weapons. The "stupidity and corruption of the Indian Bureau" encouraged the tribes to continue their fight. Greed and mismanagement were rampant. Within this environment, the Army had to protect the settlers and to pacify the rebellious tribes. Charles King (Class of 1866) wrote the story in his many widely read books on the American Indian.

Hugh L. Scott (Class of 1876) studied Indian languages for twenty years. He lived with the tribes, learned their customs and studied their inter-tribal sign language. Scott was a valuable arbitrator with the tribes and rehabilitated Geronimo at Ft. Sill. In 1898, he was assigned to the Bureau of Ethnology to conduct Indian research and to further develop the sign language. Later, he had an important role in governing Cuba and negotiated with the Moros in the Philppines. Scott became Superintendent of the Academy in 1906 and Chief of Staff of the Army in 1914.

"The greatest Indian fighter of them all" was George Crook (Class of 1852). He fought the Sioux and Cheyenne in the Black Hills during the campaigns of 1875 to 1877, where five troops of the 7th U.S.Cavalry under George A. Custer (Class of 1861) were annihilated at the Little Big Horn by Sioux under Chief Crazy Horse. Custer was buried at West Point. In 1882, Crook was ordered to return Geronimo to the San Carlos reservation. A Chiricahua Apache called "The Power", Geronimo fought for 40 years from sanctuaries in the Sierra Madre Mountains with warriors who could move 100 miles in a day. He resisted Crook for four years, finally surrendering in September, 1886. When Crook died in 1890, Sioux Chief Red Cloud said,"...he had never lied to us. His words gave the people hope." - a tribute to a respected foe!

Henry Martyn Robert

Robert's Rules of Order

"Where there is no law, but every man does what is right in his own eyes, there is the least of liberty." So said and thought Henry Martyn Robert (Class of 1857), whose political literary effort has been recognized by the printing of nearly *four million* copies of one of his books. An engineer officer whose duties placed him in contact with numerous communities and their assemblies throughout the country, Robert concluded that there was a great need for a common guide on parliamentary law and procedures. In 1874, he began to write a parliamentary manual which was "based, in its general principles, upon the rules and practices of Congress, and adapted, in its details, to the use of ordinary societies." Robert's book covered the organization and conduct of meetings, the duties of officers, the names of motions, the order of precedence for motions and the rules pertaining to motions.

Robert had great difficulty finding a publisher even though he had 4,000 ready-printed copies. To secure a contract, he had to pay for the book bindings and to "give away 1,000 copies of the book to parliamentarians, educators, legislators and church leaders." *Robert's Rules of Order* was first published on February 19, 1876, and sold out in four months. Robert died in 1923 - but his "parliamentary order" book is widely used at formal meetings across the country.

THE MAKING OF LEADERS

CHARACTER

Honor and Discipline

Alexander R. Nininger, Jr.

John M. Schofield

Sylvanus Thayer believed that "*All training for the military profession is useless without character building.*" Honor and discipline are essential in military leaders and the Cadet Honor Code states that "*a cadet will not lie, cheat or steal nor tolerate those who do.*" The necessity for the "integrity in both word and deed" of an army officer was explicitly stated by Superintendent Maxwell D. Taylor (Class of 1922), when he said that the honor system is "an essential element in the character moulding which goes on at the Military Academy" and noted, "No great soldier ever rose to eminence as a military commander, who was not primarily a man of character."

The Cadet Honor Committee meets in Nininger Hall - "*dedicated to the perpetuation of the Cadet Honor Code.*" It was gifted in memory of Alexander R. Nininger, Jr., by his 1941 classmates. Nininger was awarded the *first* Medal of Honor in World War II. He was killed on Bataan in the Philippines, while wounded and engaging the enemy in hand-to-hand combat with his rifle, bayonet and hand grenades. Nininger Hall is located in the 1st Division of Barracks.

Cadets are required to memorize *Schofield's Definition of Discipline*, which reads in part: "The discipline which makes the soldiers of a free country reliable in battle is not to be gained by harsh or tyrannical treatment. On the contrary, such treatment is far more likely to destroy than to make an army. ... He who feels the respect which is due to others cannot fail to inspire in them regard for himself..." John M. Schofield (Class of 1853), Superintendent, 1879.

CHARACTER

Cadet Chapel

Chapel of the Most Holy Trinity

Jewish Chapel

Spiritual Growth

The United States Military Academy encourages the spiritual growth of cadets as an important part of their character development. Assigned chaplains conduct services in the Protestant, Catholic and Jewish faiths and supervise a broad religious program of cadet activities that include weekend retreats, discussion groups, daily Mass and chapel services, Bible studies, choirs and Sunday school.

Catholics attend the Chapel of the Most Holy Trinity, built in 1900 and enlarged in 1949. It's architecture is Norman Gothic and it accommodates 550 cadets. Jewish cadets worship in the new 250-seat Jewish Chapel. This beautiful granite chapel was funded by private donations and contains a library and museum. It faces east toward the Hudson River and overlooks the Plain.

Protestants and Orthodox cadets worship in the Cadet Chapel - a majestic, modified-Gothic military cathedral, completed in 1911 on commanding ground above the Plain. On the chapel's east and west walls are stone carvings depicting the Crusaders, Camelot and Arthurian legends. A two-handled Crusader sword is imbedded in a cross over the main entrance doors. Inscribed in Latin on the door hinges is the phrase, "O God, who dost crush out war and by Thy powerful defense dost defeat the assailants of them that trust in Thee, come to the help of Thy servants who implore Thy mercy." The Cadet Chapel seats 1,500 cadets and houses the *largest* church organ in the world. There are 150 stained glass windows - gifts from graduated classes.

THE CADET PRAYER

O God, our Father, Thou Searcher of human hearts, help us draw near to Thee in sincerity and truth. May our religion be filled with gladness and may our worship of Thee be natural.

Strengthen and increase our admiration for honest dealing and clean thinking, and suffer not our hatred of hypocrisy and pretense ever to diminish.

Encourage us in our endeavor to live above the common level of life.

Make us to choose the harder right instead of the easier wrong, and never to be content with a half truth when the whole can be won.

Endow us with courage that is born of loyalty to all that is noble and worthy, that scorns to compromise with vice and injustice and knows no fear when truth and right are in jeopardy.

Guard us against flippancy and irreverence in the sacred things of life.

Grant us new ties of friendship and new opportunities of service.

Kindle our hearts in fellowship with those of a cheerful countenance, and soften our hearts with sympathy for those who sorrow and suffer.

Help us to maintain the honor of the Corps untarnished and unsullied, and to show forth in our lives the ideals of West Point in doing our duty to Thee and to our Country.

All of which we ask in the name of the Great Friend and Master of all.

- AMEN

CHARACTER

Heritage and Pride

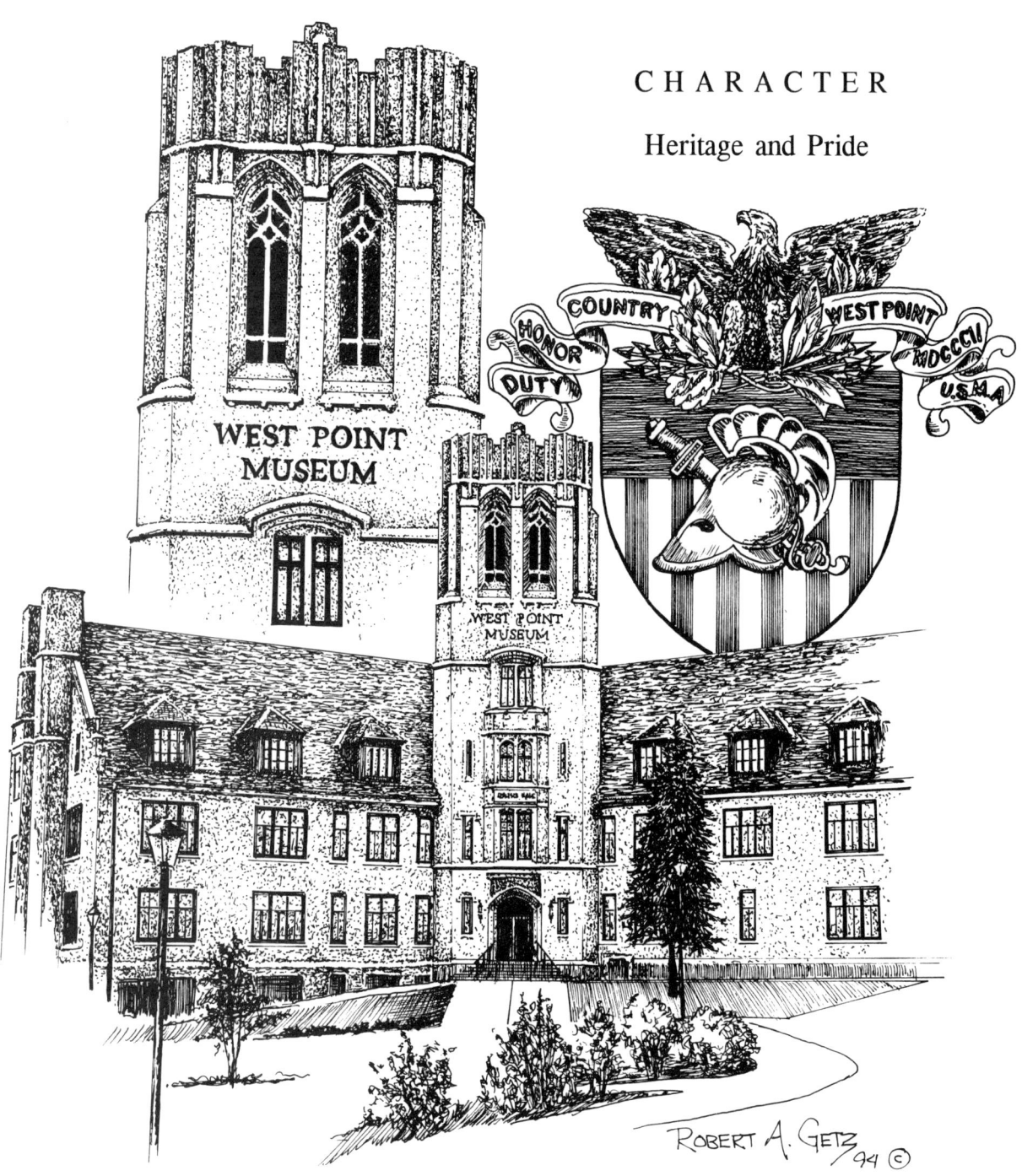

Heritage and institutional pride play important roles in the development of a cadet's character, and both are rooted in the traditions and accomplishments of *The Long Gray Line*. Some of this heritage is on display in the West Point Museum, which is one of the finest military museums in the country. Its memorabilia and the many interesting and attractive displays are a constant reminder of the Military Academy's heritage, and inspire an unparalleled degree of institutional pride. Original museum collections date back to captured British weapons from the Battle of Saratoga in 1779. There are six museum galleries with exhibits that include the histories of weapons technology, the Military Academy and the U.S. Army. The museum is located in Olmstead Hall at Pershing Center, near the Visitors Center south of Thayer Gate. Inside the museum building is the Daughters of the United States Army Gift Shop, offering visitors a wide selection of West Point memorabilia.

BENNY HAVENS, OH!

Come fill your glasses fellows,
                    and stand up in a row.
To singing sentimentally
                    we're going for to go.

In the Army there's sobriety,
                    promotion's very slow.
So we'll sing our reminiscences
                    of Benny Havens, Oh!

To our kind old Alma Mater,
                    our rockbound highland home,
We'll cast back many a fond regret
                    as o'er life's sea we roam.

Until on our last battlefield
                    the light of heaven shall glow,
We'll never fail to drink to her
                    and Benny Havens, Oh!

May the army be augmented,
                    may promotion be less slow.
May our country in the hour of need
                    be ready for the foe.

May we find a soldier's resting place
                    beneath a soldier's blow,
With room enough beside our graves
                    for Benny Havens, Oh!

CHORUS

Oh! Benny Havens, Oh!, Oh! Benny Havens, Oh!
We'll sing our reminiscences of Benny Havens, Oh!

                            - Lieutenant O'Brien

The Spanish American War

Cadet John J. Pershing

"Fighting Joe" Wheeler

A weak President, a belligerent Congress and a *yellow press* agitating against Spaniards accused of torturing rebel prisoners were a ready recipe for war and a diversion from the nation's financial problems. In February, 1898, the battleship *Maine* accidentally exploded in Havana harbor. "Remember the Maine" became the rallying call as 200,000 volunteers rushed to enlist when Congress declared war in April - but the nation was unprepared!

Congress had shortchanged the Army for years. The artillery was obsolete and the infantry were armed with old Springfield rifles with half the range of the Spanish Mausers. Troops were equipped with winter clothing in hot southern camps. Food supplies were tainted and rampant typhoid, scarlet fever, pneumonia and "yellow jack" decimated units. Deaths from disease were thirteen times those from battle. In spite of these handicaps, graduates prevailed.

An army expeditionary force landed in Cuba in June and the Spanish capitulated in mid-July. A month later they surrendered the city of Manila in the Philippines. Following the Battle of San Juan Hill in Cuba, John J. Pershing (Class of 1886), a lieutenant in an all-negro cavalry regiment, wrote, "White regiments, black regiments, regulars and Rough Riders...fought together unmindful of race or color...mindful only of their common duty as Americans." A corps commander, "Fighting Joe" Wheeler (Class of 1859), had held the same position in the Confederate Army. As the Spanish broke at Las Guasimas, he shouted, "Give it to them lads. We got the damn Yankees on the run!" - Good order, wrong war!

The Treaty of Paris was signed in December. Cuba was liberated and the Philippines were purchased for $20 million. The nation praised West Point's contribution and President "Teddy" Roosevelt, leader of the Rough Riders at San Juan Hill, said, "*...no other educational institution in the land has contributed so many names as West Point to the honor roll of the nation's greatest citizens.*" Secretary of War Root added, "*No army inspired by the spirit of the Military Academy can ever endanger a country's liberty or can ever desert its country's flag.*"

Dennis Mahan Michie

Michie Stadium

Among the graduates who lost their lives in the Spanish American War was Dennis Mahan Michie (Class of 1892) - shot at San Juan Hill on July 1, 1898. As a cadet in 1890, Michie coached and captained the *first* football team at West Point. In 1924, Michie Stadium was built and dedicated to his memory. The stadium overlooks Lusk Reservoir and is "one of the most scenic places in the U.S. to watch a college football game." It seats 40,000 spectators.

Michie's father, Peter S. Michie (Class of 1863), was a protegé of Dennis H. Mahan. He was Professor of Natural and Experimental Philosophy and was an eminent scientist in his own right. The closeness of his relationship with Mahan was evidenced in the naming of his son, Dennis Mahan Michie. Three years after Dennis was slain at San Juan Hill, Peter Michie passed away at West Point. He was the last of the three great "shapers" - *Thayer, Mahan and Michie.*

Theodore Roosevelt

George Goethals

Building the Panama Canal

While numerous graduates engineered and built canals, the greatest achievement was by George Goethals (Class of 1880), appointed in 1907 by President Theodore Roosevelt to be the chairman and chief engineer of the Panama Canal Commission. Goethals took over the nearly moribund project and completed it seven years later, when the first ship navigated the passage on August 15, 1914. Goethals drove his small army of 43,000 employees and dependents sixteen hours a day for six days a week and held staff meetings on Sundays. His "taskmaster" reputation was well deserved - but it got results. Under his leadership the channels were dredged and the locks, dams, docks, piers, power plants and fortifications were built. Goethals succeeded where others less persistent had either failed or given up. He had joined the Pacific and Atlantic Oceans - *an exceptionally important economic and military event for the United States!*

The World at War

John "Black Jack" Pershing

General of the Armies John "Black Jack" Pershing (Class of 1886) was a remarkable soldier. As a cadet he was First Captain and Class President. He fought the Spanish at San Juan Hill and the Moros in the Philippines. He was an observer of the Russo-Japanese War and pursued Pancho Villa into Mexico in 1916. While in Japan, Pershing was promoted directly from captain to brigadier general. He was a protegé of both Hugh Scott (Class of 1876) and Tasker Bliss (Class of 1875), whose careers were closely linked over many years. Both of these officers later became Chief of Staff of the Army and both recommended that Pershing lead the American Expeditionary Forces (A.E.F.) in World War I. After the war, Bliss would devote his energies to foreign relations and would help to *found* the Council on Foreign Relations.

Congress declared war on Germany on April 6, 1917. The Selective Service Act was passed in mid-May and Pershing sailed for France to prepare for the arrival of his troops. Promoted to full general, he addressed the contentious problem of whether to commit American troops piecemeal in support of Allies who had been fighting for three years, or to commit them in their own sector under American leadership. Pershing insisted on the latter and he was supported by Bliss, President Wilson's representative on the policy setting Supreme War Council.

The A.E.F. grew to 42 divisions and 1,400,000 soldiers. Their first action was at Cantigny on May 28th. This was followed by engagements at Chateau-Thierry and Belleau Wood, where two divisions repulsed strong German attacks. By mid-1918, seven divisions were present for duty and Pershing was now ready to concentrate the American force. He said to a "pale and shaking" Marshall Foch, "*While our army will fight wherever you decide, it will not fight except as an independent American Army.*" The issue was finally settled and the St.-Mihiel offensive began on September 12th with 500,000 A.E.F. soldiers in a double envelopment and linkup to eliminate a German salient. Two weeks later, the battle of the Meuse-Argonne was fought and won with 1,200,000 A.E.F. troops. Pershing then crossed the Meuse River with an Army Group, attacked toward Metz and broke the Hindenburg Line. The Germans agreed to an armistice that took effect on November 11th, 1918 - Armistice Day - now known as Veterans Day.

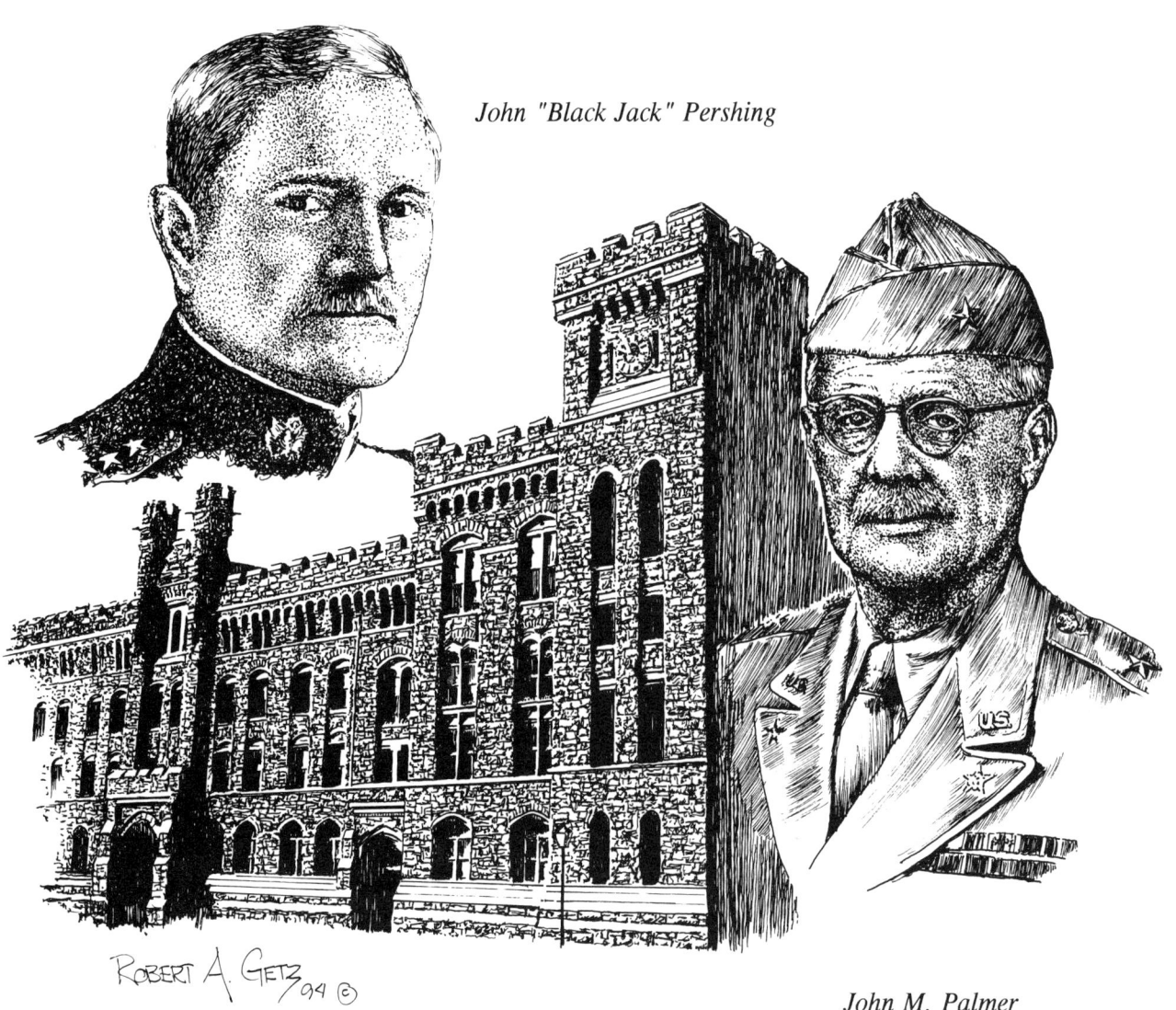

John "Black Jack" Pershing

John M. Palmer

Pershing Barracks

In 1920, the National Defense Act was passed, establishing the first adopted U.S. military policy. John M. Palmer's (Class of 1892) experience and counsel were highly influential in the coordination and passage of the Act. His presentations to the Senate Foreign Relations Committee were so impressive that the committee requested that Palmer be assigned as its official military advisor. For the *first* time the roles of the Regular Army, the National Guard and the Organized Reserves were clearly defined - but Congress failed to appropriate implementing funds. Various international pacts and treaties had "forced the possibility of war out of the national consciousness." Army Chief of Staff Pershing said to Congress, "Our Regular Army is cut too much for safety." His plea fell on deaf ears, because the "war to end all wars" was over!

After the war, Marshall Foch addressed the Corps at West Point: "*I know your motto, Duty, Honor, Country. Your graduates lived up to this motto on the battlefields, and you will do the same.*" Pershing said, the Academy "*justified itself a hundred times over in furnishing...the splendid men who have served...in the old West Point Spirit.*" In 1959, the West Academic Building bordering Central Area was converted and renamed Pershing Barracks and the Museum and the Visitors Center are both now located at Pershing Center, south of Thayer Gate.

Scientist George O. Squier

George O. Squier (Class of 1887) studied under Professor Peter Michie at West Point. In 1882, Michie had published *Elements of Wave Motion, Relating to Sound and Light* - an important step toward modern electronics theory and a subject of great interest to Squier. While serving as director of the Signal Corps' Aeronautical Division, Squier became the *first* American aircraft passenger in September, 1907, flying in a Wright brothers demonstration at Ft. Myer, Virginia. In December of that year he drafted the *first* specifications for an army airplane.

Squier earned his Ph.D with off-duty study at Johns Hopkins University, where he concentrated on the development of electrical communication technology. On January 3, 1911, he received four patents for the "Squier standard multiplex system" that permitted ten or more multiple and simultaneous two-way conversations over one electrical circuit. In 1930, he invented the "monophone," which permitted radio and the telephone to be interfaced. Squier was awarded many honors. He was a Johns Hopkins University Fellow and was *twice* presented the Franklin Institute Medal, awarded "for international scientific achievement." When Squier died in 1934, he had "*won recognition as one of the world's outstanding scientists.*"

THE MAKING OF LEADERS

PHYSICAL TRAINING

"Upon the fields of friendly strife are sown the seeds, that upon other fields on other days, will bear the fruits of victory." Douglas MacArthur (Class of 1903) knew that the stress of battle required physically fit officers. While Superintendent in 1920, he instituted an intramural sports program and challenged cadets with *"every man an athlete."* All cadets are taught swimming, gymnastics and close quarters combatives. The men also receive instruction in boxing and wrestling, while the women receive self defense instruction. Every cadet is also required to learn two "lifetime" sports. A post World War II study of general officers by Professor James Howerton of George Washington University concluded that "There is a high positive relationship between participation in athletics and display of leadership traits as cadets and future success in the Army."

The Corps of Cadets is organized into regiments for intramural sports. Cadet companies participate in a wide range of major and minor sports, with the coaching and officiating being performed by selected upperclass cadets. Club Sports include bowling, cycling, crew, fencing, sailing, sport parachute, equestrian, karate and judo, skeet and trap and marathon. These teams compete nationally and have produced many team and individual championships. Hobby Club Sports include hunting, fishing, archery, scuba diving, mountain climbing and skiing.

Crandall Natatorium is one of the finest 50 meter pools in the East with eight lanes, two diving platforms, four diving boards and seating for 1,250 spectators. Robert Crandall (Class of 1939), a swimming team captain, was killed near the end of World War II. His memorial pool is located in the gymnasium complex behind the Superintendent's Quarters.

PHYSICAL TRAINING

MacArthur Memorial

"Every Cadet an Athlete"

PHYSICAL TRAINING

Richard T. Shea

Intercollegiate Sports

Army teams participate in over twenty-five intercollegiate sports, including football, baseball, basketball, lacrosse, track, hockey, gymnastics, wrestling, swimming, tennis, golf, pistol and rifle, squash and softball. The teams are funded by the non-profit Army Athletic Association, which derives most of its revenue from the football program. Baseball, invented by Abner Doubleday (Class of 1842), is one of the oldest Military Academy sports, dating to the Civil War. Many Army teams and individuals have won national recognition. Recently, Kevin Houston (Class of 1987) was All-American in basketball; Ann Wycoff (Class of 1989) held four NCAA swimming titles; Dennis Semmel (Class of 1987) and David Nerove (Class of 1988) were All-American wrestlers; and John Van Sant (Class of 1987) was an NCAA breaststroke champion. However, the real story of West Point athletes is one of valor and heroism in the service of their country.

One such athlete was Richard T. Shea (Class of 1952), a star long distance track and cross country runner and team captain. He was a Heptagonals champion for three years and a cross country IC4-A champion. He was also a champion on the battlefield. After graduation, Shea refused an opportunity to compete in the Olympics. Instead, he answered the call of *Duty, Honor, Country* and went to war in Korea with his classmates. There, he fought on Pork Chop Hill. For two nights and a day he led three counterattacks against the enemy, engaging in hand-to-hand combat with his carbine and grenades. He killed two enemy soldiers with a trench knife. Wounded while leading a second counterattack, he was killed in hand-to-hand combat during the third counterattack. His company commander said, "*I have never seen such courage displayed by any man.*" Richard Shea was awarded the Medal of Honor for "heroism above and beyond the call of duty." Today, the Army track team competes on the same track used by "Dick" Shea when he set five Military Academy track records - it's now named Shea Stadium.

PHYSICAL TRAINING

Football at West Point

Donald Holleder

In describing the 1988 Army-Navy game, Brent Musburger of CBS Sports said, "we look toward excellence, excellence of character exhibited in the most American of all rivalries, the Army-Navy game... the greatest rivalry in all sports." Football is very special at West Point, but its real value, as with many other competitive sports, is best measured by the development of leadership and character. As the 1936 Heisman Trophy runnerup, Charles "Monk" Meyer (Class of 1937), said with intense emotion, "The perseverance, the determination and the camaraderie that I experienced as a team player for West Point will never be out of my soul."

There have been scores of Army football All-Americans: *six* were on the 1944 team, *"perhaps the finest football team in history"*; John Trent (Class of 1950) - killed in the Korean conflict; and recently, Donald Smith (Class of 1986) and Michael Mayweather (Class of 1991). Twenty-three West Pointers are in the National Football Foundation Hall of Fame, including Felix "Doc" Blanchard and Glenn Davis (1947 Classmates); Arnold Galiffa (Class of 1950); Peter Dawkins (Class of 1959); William Carpenter (Class of 1960); and Earl Blaik (Class of 1920) - Army's head coach from 1941 to 1958. Three Blaik men won the Heisman Trophy - Davis, Blanchard and Dawkins. "Red" Blaik had six undefeated seasons and nationally dominant teams.

One of Blaik's players was All-American end Donald Holleder (Class of 1956), a true team player, who at Blaik's request in 1955 selflessly switched to quarterback. In late 1967, he again selflessly put the team first in Vietnam and went to the aid of wounded troops pinned down by heavy enemy fire. Landing at the "hot spot," he was killed while trying to rescue his soldiers. In 1985, Don Holleder joined his coach "Red" Blaik in the National Football Foundation Hall of Fame. The Holleder Multi-Purpose Sports Complex is located next to Michie Stadium. It houses the hockey and basketball teams in Tate Rink and Christl Arena. Joseph Tate (Class of 1941) and Frederick Tate (Class of 1942) were hockey playing brothers and Charles Christl, Jr. (Class of 1944) co-captained the basketball team. All three were killed in World War II.

ARMY BLUE
(the song of the Class of 1865)

We've not much longer here to stay,
                For in a month or two,
We'll bid farewell to "Kaydet Gray,"
                And don the "Army Blue."

With pipe and song we'll jog along,
                Till this short time is through,
And all among our jovial throng,
                Have donned the Army Blue.

Twas the song we sang in old plebe camp,
                When first our Gray was new.
The song we sang on summer nights,
                The song of Army Blue.

Now fellows, we must say good-bye,
                We've stuck our four years thru,
Our future is a cloudless sky,
                We'll don the Army Blue.

To the men and women of the Corps
                Who've seen their four years thru,
The work was hard, they did their part
                And all for the Army Blue.

CHORUS

Army Blue, Army Blue, Hurrah for the Army Blue,
We'll bid farewell to "Kaydet Gray" and don the "Army Blue."

                              - L.W. Becklaw

Franklin D. Roosevelt

Hugh S. Johnson

Francis C. Harrington

Phillip B. Fleming

Preparing for World War II

The "Thirties" arrived with bank failures, massive unemployment and food lines. The Army suffered from lack of manpower, funds for training and a pacifist Congress. Germany was rearming; Japan seized Manchurian and Chinese ports; Italy attacked Ethiopia; and the League of Nations was an impotent distraction. President Franklin D. Roosevelt had little foreign affairs support in Congress and the Selective Service Act passed by only *one vote* in the House of Representatives in 1940. Within this environment, Roosevelt turned to the military for help and West Pointers made many valuable contributions on the domestic front.

In 1934, Roosevelt created the National Recovery Administration with Hugh S. Johnson (Class of 1903) at its helm and classmate George A. Lynch as its executive officer. The NRA's mission was to permit a degree of industrial organization and collective bargaining between labor and industry. In 1936, Francis C. Harrington (Class of 1909) joined Roosevelt's lieutenant, Harry Hopkins, as chief engineer and later deputy of the Works Progress Administration. He next became Administrator and Commissioner of Works Projects, with the mission of constructing such important strategic facilities as airports, roads and bridges - projects that involved many graduates. In 1933, Philip B. Fleming (Class of 1911) became the deputy to Harold Ickes, Secretary of the Interior, at the Public Works Administration. Then, in 1941 he headed the Federal Works Agency and in 1949 became chairman of the Maritime Commission.

As war approached, Hopkins tapped James H. Burns (Class of 1908) as his executive officer in the founding of the Lend Lease Administration, created primarily to aid Great Britain in its war against Germany. Also recruited were George R. Spalding (Class of 1901) heading up production and Sidney P. Spalding (Class of 1912) heading up storage and shipping. Hopkins and Burns then created the Munitions Assignments Board in September, 1941. Industry was now mobilizing! Roosevelt, his lieutenants, the Army and Military Academy graduates were creating the industrial foundations necessary for defending the nation.

War in the Pacific

War came with a vengeance on December 7, 1941, "a date that will live in infamy," at Pearl Harbor, where Japanese naval warplanes struck with surprise and overwhelming force. Within days Japanese troops had landed in the Philippines. A stunned Congress, looking west to the crippled fleet at Pearl Harbor and east to a flaming Europe, declared war on the Axis Powers - Germany, Italy and Japan.

"*Sui generis, the greatest Captain of his age.*" Douglas MacArthur (Class of 1903) was awarded thirteen medals for heroism, including the Medal of Honor, in a military career that spanned half a century. He was brilliant, controversial, sensitive and a great strategist. Charming and strong willed, he was called the "*most gifted man-at-arms this nation has produced.*" Another said, he's "*the greatest leader, the greatest commander, the greatest hero in American history.*" Jonathan M. Wainwright (Class of 1906), commander on Corregidor and a prisoner for four years, said, "*I'd follow that man...anywhere...blindfolded.*" As a cadet, MacArthur was *first* in scholarship and cadet rank. In 1914, he went on a secret reconnaissance behind Mexican lines at Vera Cruz. Discovered three times, he killed seven of the enemy with a derringer pistol. In WW I, he commanded the 42nd "Rainbow" Division, receiving nine decorations for heroism. While Superintendent at West Point after WW I, he created the Cadet Honor Committee, the intramural sports program, a military efficiency rating system for cadets and made numerous curriculum changes. As Army Chief of Staff from 1930-1935, he was called the "Master Builder" and fought hard for Army manpower and resources, while preparing for a war that few anticipated. He then retired and for five years worked to build a strong Philippine army.

Far East Commander Douglas MacArthur

Superintendent MacArthur

In 1941, MacArthur was recalled to active duty as the U.S. Far East Commander. The Japanese invasion of the Philippines was tenaciously opposed by his much smaller force, trading space for valuable time and seriously delaying the enemy. Ordered to Australia, he planned and executed a brilliant Pacific campaign strategy. The world celebrated as MacArthur waded ashore at Luzon. He had made good on his promise - "I shall return." In three years, he had conquered a tough and determined enemy, while sustaining fewer total casualties than were incurred in the Battle of the Bulge - truly remarkable! Like Grant, he was determined, when he said to Robert Eichelburger (Class of 1909), "Bob,...I want you to take Buna, or not come back alive." Like Lee, he was a great strategist, fighting with boldness, ingenuity and imagination.

Statesman - Philosopher

Douglas MacArthur

MacArthur received Japan's unconditional surrender on September 2, 1945, on the deck of the battleship *USS Missouri*. He was appointed Supreme Commander for the Allied Powers (SCAP) and began to build a new Japan with a democratic constitution, land reform, labor unions, women's rights and civil liberties. MacArthur reshaped Japan's politics, economy and culture with an "iron fist in a velvet glove." He was always sensitive to the dignity of the Japanese people and his name is still beloved, respected and revered in Japan.

In 1950, when North Korea invaded South Korea, MacArthur again went to war as the *first* United Nations commander. A daring amphibious landing at Inchon in mid-September turned the tide. Seoul was recaptured and Pyongyang, the enemy capital, fell in October. Thrusting far into North Korea, he was attacked by Chinese forces in late November. He proposed widening the war by bombing "sanctuaries" in China, but Washington refused. Like Dennis Mahan, a full century earlier, MacArthur believed that, "*once war is forced upon us...apply every available means to bring it to a swift end.*" In April, 1951, the political impasse ended when MacArthur was ordered home. A grateful American people and the Congress gave him a hero's welcome.

General of the Army Douglas MacArthur was awarded the Sylvanus Thayer Medal in 1962. He said at that time, "*...your mission...is to win wars...there is no substitute for victory...if you lose, the Nation will be destroyed...The long gray line has never failed us. Were you to do so, a million ghosts in olive drab, in brown khaki, in blue and gray, would rise up from the white crosses thundering those magic words: Duty, Honor, Country,...But always in our ears ring the ominous words of Plato, that wisest of philosophers: 'Only the dead have seen the end of war.'*" The Douglas MacArthur Memorial is located on the Plain near the Superintendent's Quarters. The bronze statue of MacArthur was dedicated on September 12, 1969.

Dwight D. Eisenhower

The Great Crusade

Dwight David Eisenhower (Class of 1915) led the "Great Crusade" to liberate Europe. He was exceptionally popular and was a highly respected leader, whose broad and engaging smile endeared him to both his soldiers and to the world. Chosen for the most demanding leadership job in World War II - Supreme Commander of the Allied Forces - Eisenhower was tactful yet persuasive, and forceful but flexible. He was an excellent strategist and a leader who was able to mold strong subordinates into a successful and winning team.

Eisenhower's development as a great leader was facilitated by prewar associations with many of the Army's finest officers. Early in his career, while instructing at a Tank Corps training center with George S. Patton (Class of 1909), he gained an appreciation of mechanized warfare. He became a protegé of the "brilliant" Fox Conner (Class of 1898), with whom he studied military history while stationed in Panama. Conner had been Pershing's Operations Officer in World War I and Eisenhower's study of military history later paid off at the Command and General Staff College, where he graduated *first* in his class. He was assigned to Army Chief of Staff Pershing's office and spent two years studying World War I battlefields in France - terrain he would later fight on. Then, for six years he was MacArthur's personal military assistant.

After the Louisiana maneuvers in 1941, Chief of Staff George Marshall selected Eisenhower to head the Operations Division of the General Staff and, with the outbreak of war, placed him in command of the North African landings in November, 1942 - the *first* combined British-American effort. This successful operation was soon followed by amphibious landings on Sicily and Italy. When Italy surrendered, Mark Clark's (Class of 1917) Fifth Army continued to fight against strong German resistance, while Eisenhower prepared in England for *Operation OVERLORD* - the cross-channel invasion of Europe. On June 6, 1944, nearly 3 million soldiers, sailors and airmen assaulted the French Normandy coast - the *"greatest armada in history!"*

American Hero - President

Dwight D. Eisenhower Memorial

After securing his beachheads, Eisenhower's armies penetrated the German defenses and moved rapidly to the Loire and Seine Rivers. By September, they had closed on the West Wall at the Moselle River - blitzkrieg at its finest! *Operation MARKET GARDEN* liberated Holland, but in December, under cover of bad weather, the Germans suddenly attacked in the Ardennes. Initially successful, their penetration was defeated by a skillful Allied counterattack. With the Battle of the Bulge over, Eisenhower concentrated Allied efforts on his next objective - the Rhine River. This defensive line was breached in early March by William Hoge (Class of 1916), who discovered and seized an intact bridge at Remagen. It was a great stroke of luck. "Ike" ordered, "To hell with the planners...hold that bridgehead!" Ten days later the bridge collapsed - but the army was across the Rhine! In April, Eisenhower attacked the industrial Ruhr with "*the greatest double envelopment in all military history.*" That battle destroyed the last major organized German resistance, capturing over 300,000 enemy troops. The final drive to the Elbe River and the link-up with the Soviet Army was completed in May, 1945 - "Victory in Europe!"

General of the Army Eisenhower was the Army Chief of Staff for the next three years. In 1948, he became President of Columbia University and in 1950, he took command of Supreme Headquarters Allied Powers Europe (SHAPE). His popularity was immense. Americans trusted "Ike" as few others in history. In 1952 he entered politics and was elected President, serving two terms as the nation's thirty-fourth president. In 1961, "Ike" received the Sylvanus Thayer Award.

The Dwight D. Eisenhower Memorial is located on the Plain, across from the library. The Cadet Activities Center, Eisenhower Hall, overlooks the Hudson River. It includes a 4,370 seat auditorium, second largest on the East Coast, and a 1,000 person ballroom and snack bar. The reception foyer, Crest Hall, contains many class crests and army divisional insignia.

"The Soldier's General" and His Warrior

George S. Patton, Jr. Monument

    Omar N. Bradley (Class of 1915) was Eisenhower's "right arm" and led the 12th Army Group in the "Great Crusade." He was a *"superlative military genius"* and his troops called him *"the soldier's general."* One of the great field captains of the war, Bradley helped plan and then executed the St. Lo breakout, the exploitation across France, the Rhine River crossing and the double envelopment of the Ruhr. After the war, Bradley headed the Veterans Administration and then replaced Eisenhower as the Army Chief of Staff in 1948. When the Korean War began in June, 1950, General of the Army Bradley was the nation's senior ranking military leader - Chairman of the Joint Chiefs of Staff. He received the Sylvanus Thayer Award in 1973.

    Bradley's "right arm" was George S. Patton Jr. (Class of 1909), *"one of the great captains of history"* and a true warrior general. Patton was aggressive, a strict disciplinarian and a devoted student of war. In discussing leadership, he said, "Never tell people how to do things. Tell them what to do and they will surprise you with their ingenuity." His exploitation from St. Lo to the Loire and Seine Rivers was *"the greatest armored dash the world had yet seen."* Patton's tactical brilliance was demonstrated again with a rapid 90 degree change in direction as his Third Army successfully counterattacked the German penetration in the Battle of the Bulge. His superb leadership was recognized by friend and foe alike. Eisenhower and Bradley used his talents well and it was said of him, "the lions in their dens tremble on hearing his approach." The George S. Patton Jr. Monument was erected by the friends, officers and men of units that he commanded. It was dedicated on August 19, 1950 and is located in front of the library.

Air Power's Role

Henry "Hap" Arnold

The Air Cadet Memorial

While Squier drafted the first army airplane specifications early in the 20th Century, it remained for others to "sell" the wartime role of the airplane. One of these was Henry "Hap" Arnold (Class of 1907), a leading aviation pioneer who joined the Signal Corps pilots in 1911 and fought for the recognition of airpower for thirty years. Arnold was an observer in England during the Battle of London, an experience that reenforced his support of long-range strategic bombing. When America entered the war, Arnold was Chief of the Army Air Corps and a member of the Joint Chiefs of Staff, with the world-wide responsibility for all pilots, planes and airfields. He constantly pushed for development of the next plane, even as the latest was going into production. He created the Air Transport Command for freight and passengers, the Troop Carrier Command to deliver troops and equipment near battlefields, and the Airborne Army for the battlefield insertion of combat parachute and glider forces. Robert E. Wood (Class of 1900), chairman of the board of Sears, Rocbuck & Co., assisted Arnold in the "big business" of building an air force. Arnold's bombers devastated enemy industrial and urban complexes and his fighters maintained air superiority over most of the battlefields. When Japan refused to surrender, his B-29's delivered two nuclear weapons, destroying Hiroshima and Nagasaki. Under Arnold's five-star leadership after the war, the Army Air Corps became the *United States Air Force*.

At West Point during World War II, an Air Cadet training program was established at Stewart Field, north of the Academy. The Corps was divided into Air Cadets and Ground Cadets and at graduation, the Air Cadets received their "wings" and commissions in the Army Air Corps. The Air Cadet Monument, erected by the Corps of Cadets in 1945, memorializes those cadets who lost their lives in flight training, with the inscribed name and date of death of each deceased Air Cadet. The monument is at the north end of Lusk Reservoir, near Michie Stadium.

Leslie R. Groves
Lucius D. Clay
Herman Beukema (l.to r.)

Nuclear Engineer - Governor - Educator

The destruction of Hiroshima ushered in the nuclear age. For the first time, Americans learned of the TOP SECRET "Manhattan Engineer District Project" that had created the nuclear energy industry, and its leader Leslie R. Groves (Class of Nov. 1918). In 1942, Groves was assigned responsibility for all of the project's personnel, procurement, construction and the coordination of an international team of scientists. His Executive Officer was Kenneth D. Nichols (Class of 1929), who later became the General Manager of the Atomic Energy Commission.

In June, 1948, soldier-statesman Lucius D. Clay (Class of June, 1918) was the Military Governor in West Germany when the Soviets cut off all ground traffic to West Berlin. Clay urged the Allies to stand firm in their support of West Berlin and the Berlin Airlift was born. *Operation VITTLES* supplied food and fuel to 2 1/2 million West Berliners for eleven months. At its peak, 13,000 tons were delivered daily by William H. Tunner's (Class of 1928) massive air armada. The Soviets yielded in May and an inspired Germany began to rise from the ashes of war.

At West Point, Herman Beukema (Class of 1915), geo-politician, founded a department later renamed the Department of Social Sciences. From 1930 to 1954, he added a "*new breadth and depth to the cadet's education.*" New courses included international relations, the economics of national security and contemporary foreign governments. Distinguished lecturers regularly addressed the Corps and by 1948 liberal arts courses comprised 40 percent of the curriculum. George A. Lincoln (Class of 1929) joined Beukema in 1947 and led the department from 1954 to 1969. Lincoln continued Beukema's work and published the *Economics of National Security*, a widely used textbook. Both Beukema and Lincoln were recognized as leading-edge educators.

THE MAKING OF LEADERS

EXTRACURRICULAR ACTIVITIES

Eisenhower Hall and Cullum Hall

Eisenhower Hall is an important center of cadet social life. It supports presentations by Broadway tour companies, cadet plays, Glee Club and Choir concerts and a Performing Arts Series that includes frequently scheduled opera, ballet, symphony orchestra and dance companies. A Cadet Fine Arts program sponsors visiting artists and several visual exhibitions during the academic year. The Dialectic Society's annual "100th Night Show" and productions by the Cadet Theatre Arts Guild are presented in "Ike" Hall. Dance "hops" are held in the ballroom and current-run movies are regularly shown in the large auditorium.

Cullum Hall was built in 1898 on the eastern edge of the Plain. It was gifted by George W. Cullum (Class of 1833) and dedicated *"To the deceased Officers and Graduates of the Military Academy."* The building contains a downstairs lounge and outdoor balcony that overlooks the Hudson River and an upper level ballroom. Cullum Hall is designed in the classical Greek Revival architectural style and contains numerous plaques and paintings of former superintendents, professors and graduates killed in action. Cullum was Superintendent from 1864 to 1866. He was "one of West Point's first serious historians" and published a *Biographical Register* of graduates in 1868.

EXTRACURRICULAR ACTIVITIES

Richard Delafield

Delafield Pond

On the high ground above the Plain and the chapels, nestled in the woods, is a quiet, scenic spot called Delafield Pond. On a hot summer day, one can find cadets and their dates "catching rays" and relaxing at this beautiful, secluded spring-fed lake. A large clubhouse with locker room facilities, beach area and separate platform, diving and swimming areas provide for pleasant afternoons just a short walk from the cadet barracks areas. Delafield Pond is named after Richard Delafield (Class of 1818), a three-time Superintendent at the Military Academy, including the five difficult years that immediately preceded the Civil War.

EXTRACURRICULAR ACTIVITIES

Cadet Recreation

The old adage, "We work hard and we play hard" is particularly true at West Point. Recreational facilities for extracurricular activities abound at the Academy, where over 100 activities cater to the many varied cadet interests. Water sports such as sailing, water skiing, canoeing and scuba diving are available on the Hudson River, Lake Popolopen, Round Pond, Delafield Pond and swimming pool areas. Thousands of acres of woodlands, mountains and streams offer unlimited hunting, fishing, hiking, climbing and camping opportunities. Other recreational facilities include numerous tennis courts, a superb 18-hole golf course, ski slopes, an ice skating rink, skeet and trap ranges and sports parachuting. All of these facilities are actively used by the Corps as they unwind from academics. "There's something for everybody!"

The Association of Graduates

George W. Cullum (Class of 1833) helped to *found* the Association of Graduates (AOG), which first met on May 22, 1869. Thayer was the *first* elected president. In early 1995, the AOG moved from Cullum Hall to the newly constructed James K. Herbert Alumni Center, named for James Keller Herbert (Class of 1930). This beautiful three-story Alumni Center, located near Michie Stadium on the former site of Smith Rink, provides spacious meeting rooms, lounges and a *Great Hall* for receptions. Also in the Alumni Center is the AOG Gift Shop, offering a wide selection of gifts. In 1991, the AOG, perceiving a need to honor deserving graduates, created the Distinguished Graduate Award for *"those graduates whose distinguished service clearly emulates the principles embodied in the Academy's motto, Duty, Honor, Country."* Two of the 1994 recipients were Paul W. Thompson and E. Douglas Kenna, longtime Association leaders.

Paul W. Thompson (Class of 1929) trained and commanded the special engineer troops that led the D-Day assault. When Thompson was wounded, Eisenhower placed him in charge of the *European Stars and Stripes*. After the war, he joined *Readers Digest*, becoming Executive Vice President in 1968. From 1970 to 1974, Thompson was President of the AOG, where he directed a broad reorganization of alumni support and a private fund raising program, which he later successfully led as a volunteer.

E. Douglas Kenna (Class of 1945), All-American in football and basketball, is in the National Football Hall of Fame. This "captain of industry" was President of Fuqua Industries, the National Association of Manufacturers and Carrier Corporation. He is a partner and director of Ohrstrom Group, which controls Roper Industries and the Dover and Carlisle Corporations. He has served as a trustee of universities and foundations and was named Trustee Emeritus of the AOG in 1987. "Doug" Kenna - a man of "monumental talents" and a great leader.

The Korean War

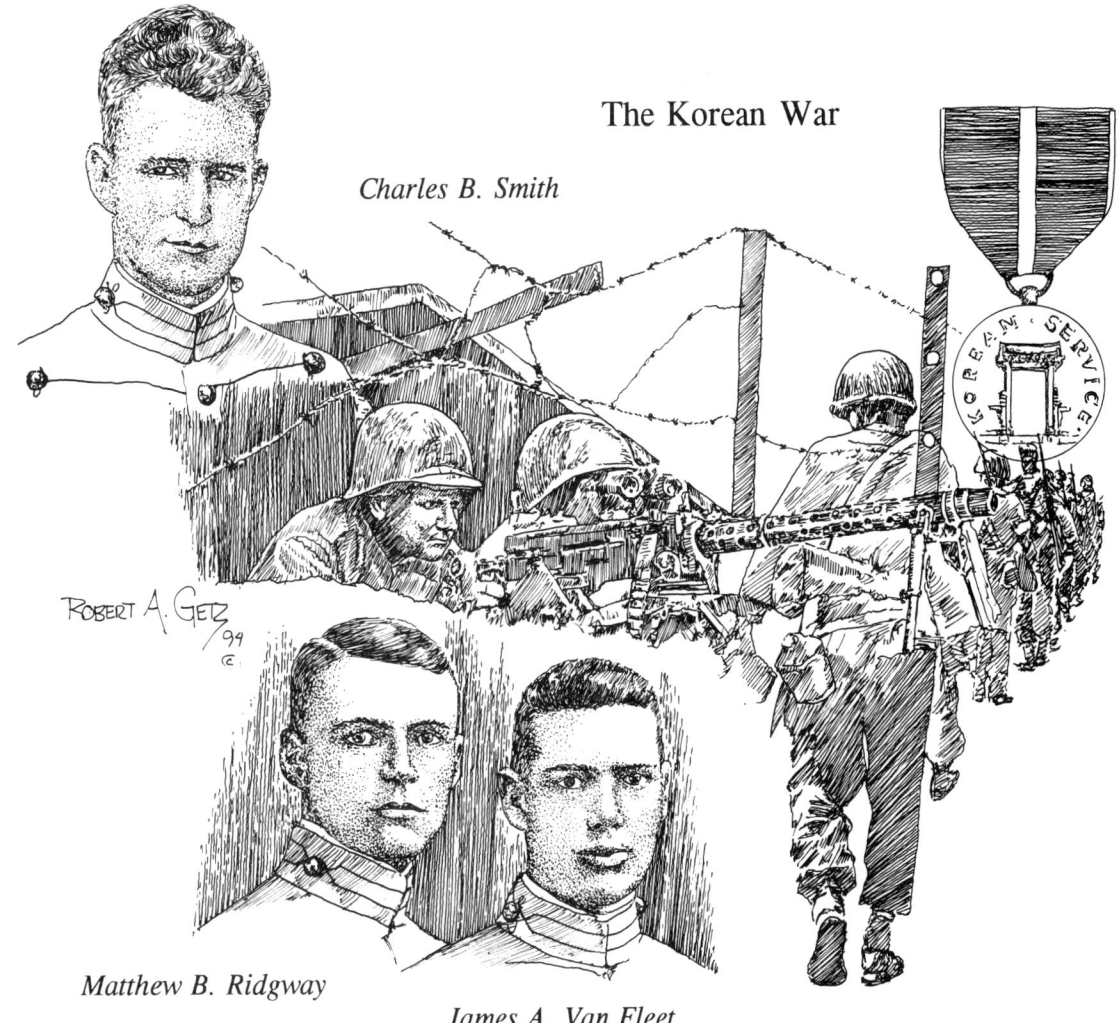

Charles B. Smith

Matthew B. Ridgway

James A. Van Fleet

"*A shocked United States once again realized - too late - what false economy does to the national security.*" Presidential envoy Albert C. Wedemeyer (Class of 1919) had warned of Soviet plans for Korea in a "long-hidden" 1947 report. One year after American combat troops withdrew to Japan, North Korea struck. Poorly equipped troops in understrength units rushed back to Korea and Charles B. Smith's (Class of 1939) task force made contact on July 4th - Independence Day. That battle is still bitterly remembered by many, in describing a Congress that too frequently forgets too soon! Task Force Smith, with no relief, was crushed in a violent four hour fight. Its survivors escaped only by abandoning their equipment. Without benefit of branch training, the specialized training that normally follows graduation, the Class of 1950 immediately filled vacant platoon leader positions in Korea. Forty-one were killed - the highest class death toll in Military Academy history. West Point battle casualties totaled 267 in this undeclared and limited war.

Eighth Army finally held and counterattacked, driving the enemy north, but a surprise "Chinese" attack in November forced the army back into defensive positions north of Seoul. The Eighth Army commander, Walton H. Walker (Class of 1912), was accidentally killed and Matthew B. Ridgway (Class of April, 1917) assumed command. Ridgway had led airborne troops during WW II, when Eisenhower had called him "*one of the finest soldiers this war has produced.*" Ridgway counterattacked and in Omar Bradley's words, his "brilliant, driving, uncompromising leadership" quickly turned the tide. When MacArthur was ordered home in 1951, Ridgway became the United Nations Supreme Commander and James A. Van Fleet (Class of 1915) took command of the Eighth Army. In WW II, Van Fleet had been a divisional and corps commander and after the war he fought communism as head of the Military Mission in Greece. Later, Ridgeway was appointed Chief of Staff of the Army and also served as the NATO commander. Ridgway and Van Fleet were each awarded the Distinguished Graduate Award in 1992. Both were highly decorated "*leaders of great intelligence, breadth and character.*"

Advisors to Presidents

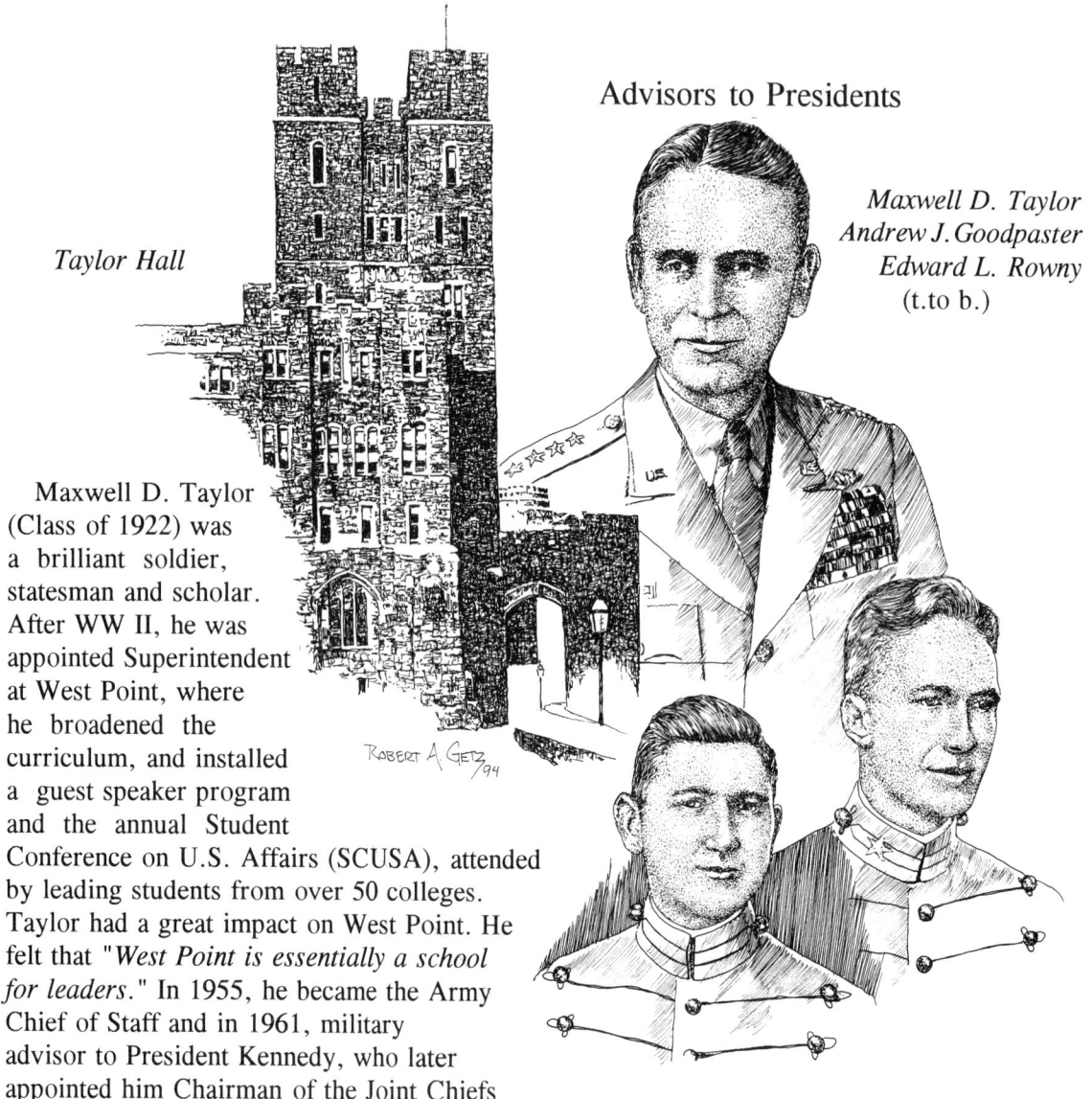

Taylor Hall

*Maxwell D. Taylor
Andrew J. Goodpaster
Edward L. Rowny
(t. to b.)*

Maxwell D. Taylor (Class of 1922) was a brilliant soldier, statesman and scholar. After WW II, he was appointed Superintendent at West Point, where he broadened the curriculum, and installed a guest speaker program and the annual Student Conference on U.S. Affairs (SCUSA), attended by leading students from over 50 colleges. Taylor had a great impact on West Point. He felt that "*West Point is essentially a school for leaders.*" In 1955, he became the Army Chief of Staff and in 1961, military advisor to President Kennedy, who later appointed him Chairman of the Joint Chiefs of Staff (JCS). In 1964, Taylor was Ambassador to South Vietnam for a year. Then for four years he served as a Special Consultant to President Johnson. The Administration Building, Taylor Hall, is reputedly America's tallest all-stone building with no steel supports - 160 feet.

Andrew J. Goodpaster (Class of 1939) advised *four* Presidents. He was military advisor to Presidents Eisenhower and Kennedy for seven years. His reputation "as the Army's most brilliant mind" led to his assignment to the Vietnam peace negotiations in Paris, while still Commandant of the National War College. He retired after commanding the NATO forces for five years. Recalled in 1977 to be Superintendent at West Point, his leadership inspired a "resurgence of the values" that have always been a hallmark of the Military Academy. In 1984, President Reagan awarded Goodpaster the Presidential Medal of Freedom and in 1992, he received the Distinguished Graduate Award. Goodpaster made a major "*contribution to the security and freedom of the United States and to the cause of peace.*"

Edward L. Rowny (Class of 1941) was decorated for heroism as a battalion commander in WW II and a regimental commander in the Korean War. From 1973 to 1979, he represented the JCS at the Strategic Arms Limitation Talks (SALT), where his negotiating skills gained him international recognition. In 1982, Rowny became the Chief U.S. Negotiator at the Strategic Arms Reduction Talks (START). He next was a Special Advisor on arms control matters to the President and Secretary of State from 1985 to 1988. President Reagan presented Rowny with the President's Citizens Medal in 1988 and in 1993, he was awarded the Distinguished Graduate Award. Rowny was "*a leading architect of American foreign policy in the field of arms control.*"

The Vietnam War

William C. Westmoreland

Southeast Asia Memorial

Creighton W. Abrams

America fought another undeclared and limited war from 1962 to 1975 - South Vietnam in Southeast Asia. For years, knowledgeable military officers had counseled against involvement in an Asian land war, but the "domino theory" was popular and our ally needed help. President John Kennedy first sent military advisors and then Special Forces troops. By 1968, President Lyndon Johnson had increased the commitment to over 530,000 troops. Whether or not to continue the war became a national crisis that finally led to Johnson's decision to not run for reelection. President Richard Nixon then presided over a withdrawal that lasted several years.

William C. Westmoreland (Class of 1936) fought with the 9th Infantry Division in WW II. In 1960, he was appointed Superintendent at West Point, serving for three years. He then commanded the 101st Airborne Division and the 18th Airborne Corps. In 1964, he assumed command of the Military Assistance Command, Vietnam (MACV), where he remained for four years. When he left, the conflict had grown from guerilla warfare into major pitched battles with North Vietnamese regular army forces. In 1968, Westmoreland became the Army Chief of Staff, a position he held for four years, and Creighton W. Abrams (Class of 1936) assumed command of MACV. Abrams had a warrior reputation in the army and was perhaps the army's leading armored warfare proponent and expert. In WW II, he had commanded a battalion and a combat command of the 4th Armored Division in Patton's Third Army, and was a highly decorated combat leader. In 1972, he succeeded Westmoreland as the Army Chief of Staff. The Southeast Asia Memorial at West Point is located at the south end of Lusk Reservoir. It was dedicated by the Classes of 1960 through 1969 to classmates and other service members who fell in Vietnam.

Frank Borman

David R. Scott

Space Age Pioneers

Edward H. White, II

    The Soviet space launch of Sputnik surprised the nation. The United States was supposed to be the world leader in science. The cry "First in Space!" swept across the land, as we began to organize for the coming space race, and a new vocabulary entered mainstream America's conversation - space capsule, earth and lunar orbit, docking, space walk, space laboratory and astronaut. West Point provided many of the highly trained astronauts in this new national crusade.

    Frank Borman (Class of 1950) commanded the *first* spacecraft rendezvous in December, 1965, and the *first* spacecraft lunar orbit in December, 1968. He went on to become the President of Eastern Airlines in 1975. Edwin "Buzz" Aldrin (Class of 1951) was a Gemini pilot and participated in the *first* manned Apollo flight to the Moon and the *first* manned Apollo Moon landing on July 20, 1969. Edward H. White II (Class of 1952) was the *first* man to walk in space in June, 1965. White subsequently lost his life in a launch-pad fire on January 27, 1967. David R. Scott (Class of 1954) was co-pilot of Gemini 8's *first* docking of two space vehicles in March, 1966, and was the commander of Apollo 15 in 1971. From 1975 to 1977, he directed the NASA Flight Research Center. Other West Point astronauts include Donald H. Peterson and Alfred M. Worden (1955 Classmates); Richard M. Mullane and Sherwood C. Spring (1967 Classmates), both recent Space Shuttle crewmen; William S. McArthur, Jr. (Class of 1973); Michael R. Clifford (Class of 1974); and Charles D. Gemar (Class of 1979), recent flight engineer on Space Shuttle Columbia. West Point's astronauts - Twentieth Century space-age pioneers!

THE ALMA MATER

Hail, Alma Mater dear,
                          To us be ever near.
Help us thy motto bear
                          Through all the years.
Let DUTY be well performed,
                    HONOR be e'er untarned,
COUNTRY be ever armed,
                          West Point by thee.

Guide us, thy sons, aright,
                          Teach us by day, by night,
To keep thine honor bright,
                          For thee to fight.
When we depart from thee,
                          Serving on land or sea,
May we still loyal be,
                          West Point, to thee.

And when our work is done,
                          Our course on earth is run,
May it be said, "Well done;
                          Be thou at peace."
E'er may that line of gray,
                          Increase from day to day,
Live, serve, and die, we pray,
                          West Point, for thee.

                                    - P.S. Reineke
                                      Class of 1911

Desert Storm

On August 2nd, 1990, Iraq invaded Kuwait, threatening Saudi Arabia and western oil supplies. President Bush declared that the hostile action "will not stand" and the United Nations Security Council demanded an Iraqi withdrawal by January 15, 1991. Iraq ignored the order and a massive air campaign began immediately. H. Norman Schwarzkopf (Class of 1956), a highly decorated veteran of Vietnam, was the field commander. His army reached full strength with the arrival of the U.S. VII Corps from Germany. A second deadline to withdraw from Kuwait was ignored by Iraq and the ground war began on the 23rd of February. It was all over in 100 hours of blitzkrieg warfare!

Schwarzkopf attacked with "*one of the most complex mechanized operations since World War II*" - an envelopment of the Iraqi right flank, followed by an encirclement and attack of the Iraqi rear. Twenty-nine enemy divisions were either destroyed or crippled and their tank forces were decimated. The deceptive battle plan included a threatened amphibious landing and a diversionary frontal attack that pinned down major enemy forces. The bulk of Schwarzkopf's armored force was shifted 100 miles to the west, where it lay hidden for 30 days, ten miles from the Saudi-Iraqi border. From those attack positions, "the greatest cavalry charge in history" was launched, sweeping 250 miles to the Euphrates River and then east to the gates of Basra. The 24th Infantry Division (Mechanized), commanded by Barry R. McCaffrey (Class of 1964), also a highly decorated Vietnam warrior, led the dash. The Republican Guard divisions were driven north and west out of Kuwait. McCaffrey's division, attacking east along the Euphrates, met the fleeing Republican Guard and closed the trap - sealing the killing zone for "a classic tank battle." The 24th Division had moved "*farther with more firepower than Patton's entire Third Army*" in World War II. On February 28th, Iraq accepted the allied coalition's terms, ending the hostilities. Kuwait was liberated. President Bush presented Schwarzkopf with the Presidential Medal of Freedom and said, "it is a time of pride in our troops." The Army had "*proved they were the best Army in the world.*" In 1994, Schwarzkopf received the Distinguished Graduate Award at West Point.

H. Norman Schwarzkopf

Barry R. McCaffrey

Graduate Pathfinders

Thoralf M. Sundt, Jr.   *Roscoe Robinson, Jr.*   *Robert F. McDermott*

Robert F. McDermott (Class of 1943), nationally recognized educator and "captain of industry," served on the faculty at West Point from 1950 to 1954. He then became the *first* Dean of Faculty at the U.S. Air Force Academy, a position he held for ten years. Retiring in 1968, he joined United Services Automobile Association (USAA) and quickly became it's Chairman. Under his leadership the small company's membership quadrupled in the next 25 years. USAA is now a world-class financial services company and Chairman Emeritus McDermott is a recognized leader in both the insurance industry and the community. He is in the Texas Business Hall of Fame and the National Business Hall of Fame and has received *five* honorary doctoral degrees. He *founded* the San Antonio Economic Development Foundation and the Texas Research and Technology Foundation, *co-founded* United San Antonio, and helped to establish the Business Careers High School. McDermott was awarded the Distinguished Graduate Award in 1993.

Roscoe Robinson, Jr. (Class of 1951) was the *first* African-American to attain four-star rank as a full general in the United States Army. He was a highly decorated battalion commander in Vietnam and served three tours with the 82nd Airborne Division, the last in 1972 as the division's commanding general. Robinson went on to command the U.S. Army in Japan and in 1980 was appointed the U.S. Representative to the NATO Military Committee. For 34 years he honored the principles of West Point and the Army with the highest possible standards of professional conduct. Robinson was awarded the Distinguished Graduate Award in 1993.

Thoralf M. Sundt, Jr. (Class of 1952) completed neurosurgery studies at the Mayo Clinic in 1964. In 1979, he became Chairman of the Department of Neurosurgery at the Mayo Clinic He *pioneered* "the use of surgical microscopes" and "invented numerous devices" used in neurosurgery. He was internationally acclaimed and his honors included: "Outstanding Alumnus" from the University of Tennessee-Memphis College of Medicine; "Distinguished Mayo Clinical Award"; and "Grass Prize and Medal" from the Society of Neurological Surgery. He was Vice-Chairman of the American Board of Neurological Surgery and editor of the *Journal of Neurosurgery*. In 1992, Sundt was awarded the Distinguished Graduate Award.

Graduate Pathfinders

Brent Scowcroft

Bernard W. Rogers   *Benjamin O. Davis, Jr.*

Three graduates received the 1995 Distinguished Graduate Award. Benjamin O. Davis, Jr. (Class of 1936) graduated with the *first* class of black airmen at Tuskegee Army Air Field in 1942 and led the *first* black air unit into combat in North Africa and Sicily, the 99th Pursuit Squadron. He then commanded the 332nd Fighter Group over Italy. After the war, Davis held many important posts, including Chief of Staff, USAF, Korea; Chief of Staff, United Nations Command, Korea; and the Deputy Commander of Strike Force Command. He retired with three stars in 1970 and then served as Assistant Secretary of Transportation, where he worked to eliminate terrorist hijacking of aircraft in the continental United States. General Davis' forty year "career exemplifies uncommon dedication to the ideal of selfless service."

Bernard W. Rogers' (Class of June, 1943) "contributions in the service of his country and to the NATO Alliance are unparalleled." After attending Oxford as a Rhodes Scholar, Rogers led an infantry battalion in combat in Korea in 1951. As an assistant division commander in Vietnam, he received the Distinguished Service Cross and as a division commander in 1969, he rehabilitated his division with programs later adopted for army-wide use in the "all-volunteer" army. He was Chief of Staff of the Army in 1976, and for *eight* years served as the NATO commander in Europe. Rogers "rendered a lifetime of extraordinary service to his country."

Brent Scowcroft (Class of 1947) served on the faculty at the Military Academy, and later at the Air Force Academy as an Associate Professor in the Political Science Department. In 1972, he became Military Assistant to the President. Retiring in 1975 as a three star general, Scowcroft was made Deputy Assistant to the President for U.S. National Security Affairs that same year, and in 1978 he became a member of the President's General Advisory Committee on Arms Control. In 1983, Scowcroft was appointed Chairman of the President's Commission on Strategic Forces, and in 1985, he joined the President's Blue Ribbon Commission on Defense Management. He participated in planning for the reunification of Germany; helped plan the Desert Storm strategy; and was a key advisor on the North American Free Trade Agreement. Scowcroft has been a "distinguished Air Force officer, educator, statesman, internationally renowned expert on global politics, and respected advisor on national security affairs to five presidents."

THE MAKING OF LEADERS

GRADUATION

Graduation Week

"How many days, Cadet?" Bracing, the Plebe shouts, "Sir, there are ten days to graduation!" Spring is in the air with sunny days, cool breezes off the Hudson River and the early morning smell of cut grass on the Plain. Graduation Week is close at hand. For the Plebes, it means their first West Point summer vacation, followed by military training at Camp Buckner. For the Yearlings, it brings summer leave and training trips. For the Cows, it means assuming leadership of the Corps and for the Firsties, it brings a lot of goodbyes and the start of a challenging army career. Every year, Graduation Week is an unforgettable and magical week!

Graduation Parade! Family and friends encircle the Plain, proudly looking for *their* cadet - dressed in Full Dress Uniform, drawn saber or rifle with fixed bayonet, crisply starched white trousers, spit-shined shoes and glistening brass. Four thousand strong, the Corps moves in perfect formation as the battalions and regiments march "on line" to the music of the *Stars and Stripes Forever* - a Corps favorite. The band then "troops the line" while playing the *Graduation March*, a series of old well-known melodies. In the ranks, Plebes are loudly reciting for the last time - "Name that march, Cadet!" "How's the cow, Cadet?" The familiar notes of *Army Blue* drift across the Plain and the First Class separates into ranks, apart from the Corps. As the band plays the *Alma Mater*, they march across the Plain, turn, and face the Corps. It's an emotional moment - sorrow at leaving, pride in accomplishment, and a renewal of purpose. Standing tall and proud, some recall those words from *The Corps* - "The long gray line of us stretches through the years of a century told and the last man feels to his marrow the grip of your far off hold." Suddenly the reverie ends as the "Pass in Review" begins to the stirring music of the *Official West Point March* - sabers flash and guidons dip to "Eyes Right" - a salute and a final goodbye to the First Class. Tomorrow is graduation and a fond farewell to "our rockbound highland home"!

THE CORPS

The Corps, Bareheaded, salute it,
          With eyes up, thanking our God -

That we of the Corps are treading
          Where they of the Corps have trod -

They are here in ghostly assemblage,
          The men of the Corps long dead,

And our hearts are standing attention
          While we wait for their passing tread.

We, sons of today we salute you -
          You, sons of an earlier day;

We follow, close order, behind you,
          Where you have pointed the way;

The long gray line of us stretches
          Through the years of a century told,

And the last man feels to his marrow
          The grip of your far off hold.

Grip hands with us now, though we see not,
          Grip hands with us, strengthen our hearts

As the long line stiffens and straightens
          With the thrill that your presence imparts.

Grip hands - though it be from the shadows -
          While we swear as you did of yore,

Or living, or dying, to honor
          The Corps, and the Corps, and the Corps.

          - Bishop H.S. Shipman
          Chaplain (1896-1905)

GRADUATION

Graduation Day

"I,... having been appointed an officer in the Army of the United States... in the grade of Second Lieutenant do solemnly swear that I will support and defend the Constitution of the United States against all enemies, foreign and domestic, that I will bear true faith and allegiance to the same;... and that I will well and faithfully discharge the duties... SO HELP ME GOD."

"Leaders of high moral character for the nation." It's Graduation Day - the culmination of four years of hard work. The speaker is well-known and talks about dedication, commitment, knowledge, character, leadership and service to country. Everyone understands - it's what West Point is all about! Suddenly, the ceremony ends - the last man has received his diploma. The First Captain orders, "Class Dismissed!" Hats are tossed high into the air. Cheers and yells sweep the crowd. New second lieutenants rush to family and friends, prepare for long awaited weddings and shout their final goodbyes. Soon, they will report to their first station - a basic branch officers school somewhere in the country.

Even as new "shavetail" second lieutenants, these young officers will soon be "in a leadership role of great importance." They all will quickly experience the challenge and satisfaction of serving their country. Each will immediately encounter broader responsibilities and greater leadership demands than most of their peers in other professions. These responsibilities will include the training, health, safety, welfare and morale of their soldiers, and the maintenance of highly technical and costly equipment in widely diverse worldwide assignments. Their breadth of education and leadership experience will make them increasingly sought after for high-level civilian leadership positions. They are a national treasure, and like others before them they will quickly demonstrate their value in war and peace. It begins at the United States Military Academy with the development of knowledge and character, and their value continues to grow through a lifetime of service to their country and to America's sons and daughters placed in their care. These young men and women guarantee the nation unmatched professionalism, character and competence, as they follow in the footsteps of *The Long Gray Line* - trusting in their motto, *Duty, Honor, Country*.

BIBLIOGRAPHY

Ambrose, Stephen E. *Duty, Honor, Country, A History of West Point*. New York: John Hopkins Press. 1966.

American Heritage. *World War I*. New York: Simon and Schuster, Inc. 1964.

Army Athletic Association. *Sports Brochures*. West Point, NY: AAA. 1994.

Association of Graduates. *The Assembly Magazine*. Various issues including 1991 (Sep & Nov); 1992 (Jan, Sep and Nov); 1993 (Jan, Mar, May and July); and 1995 (July).

Association of Graduates. *Distinguished Graduate Award Citations*. West Point, NY: 1992-1994.

Association of Graduates. *Register of Graduates*. West Point, NY: 1992 and 1993.

Baumer, William H., Jr. *West Point*. New York: D. Appleton-Century Company, Inc. 1942.

Catton, Bruce. *The American Heritage Picture History of the Civil War*. New York: American Heritage Publishing Co., Inc. 1960.

Dupuy, R. Ernest. *Men of West Point*. New York: William Sloane Associates. 1951.

Fleming, Thomas J. *West Point, The Men and Times of the United States Military Academy*. New York: William Morrow & Co., Inc. 1969.

Freeman, Douglas Southall. *R.E. Lee*. New York: Charles Scribners Sons. 1934.

Greely, Horace. *The American Conflict, A History of the Great Rebellion in the U.S.A., Vol I*. Chicago: O.D. Case & Co. 1865.

Hackworth, David and Julie Sherman. *About Face*. New York: Simon and Schuster, Inc. 1989.

MacArthur, Douglas. *Reminiscences*. New York: McGraw-Hill Book Company. 1964.

Manchester, William. *American Caesar*. New York: Little Brown & Co. 1978.

Moore, Harold G. and Joseph L. Galloway. *We Were Soldiers Once*. New York: Random House, Inc. 1992.

NASA Public Relations. *Spinoff 1992* and Miscellaneous Summaries and Articles. 1994.

Pappas, George S. *The Cadet Chapel, USMA (Revised) Fourth Edition*. West Point, NY: 1983.

Patterson, Gerard A. *Rebels from West Point*. New York: Doubleday & Co. 1987.

Reeder, Red. *The West Point Story*. New York: Random House. 1956

Ridpath, John C. *History of the United States*. Chicago: C.B. Beach & Co. 1877.

Robert, Henry Martyn. *Robert's Rules of Order (Revised)*. Glenview, Ill: Scott Foresman and Co. 1970.

Sheehan, Neil. *A Bright and Shining Lie*. New York: Random House, Inc. 1988.

Simpson, Henry. *Officers and Gentlemen*. Tarreytown, NY: Sleepy Hollow Press. 1982.

Smith, Gene. *Lee and Grant*. New York: McGraw Hill & Co. 1984.

United States Military Academy. *Candidate Informational Publications*. West Point, NY: Admissions Department. 1993.

United States Military Academy. *Bugle Notes*. West Point, NY: USMA. 1950.

United States Military Academy. *Bugle Notes*. West Point, NY: USMA. 1992-1996.

United Services Automobile Association. *A Tradition of Service* and *McDermott Biography*. San Antonio, TX: USAA. 1994.

Washington Post Newspaper. *Columbia Shuttle* (3-5-94) and *Matthew Ridgeway* (7-27-93).

Woodward, Bob. *The Commanders*. New York: Simon and Schuster, Inc. 1991.